A Plea for Common Sense

A Plea for Common Sense

Resolving the Clash between Religion and Politics

Jim Castelli

Foreword by Norman Lear

A People for the American Way Book

1817

Harper & Row Publishers, San Francisco
Cambridge, Hagerstown, New York, Philadelphia, Washington
London, Mexico City, São Paulo, Singapore, Sydney

FIRST EDITION

Library of Congress Cataloging-in-Publication Data

Castelli, Jim.
    A plea for common sense.

    "A People for the American way book."
    Bibliography: p.
    Includes index.
    1. Religion and politics—United States. 2. United States—Politics and government—1981–   . 3. United States—Religion—1960–
4. Conservatism—United States—History—20th century. I. Title.
BL2525.C37   1988   322'.1'0973   87-45693
ISBN 0-06-016324-6

88 89 90 91 92 RRD 10 9 8 7 6 5 4 3 2 1

Contents

Foreword

By Norman Lear

It was my grandfather—tall, slender, proud, straight as a die—who taught me the meaning of citizenship. He used to write the president. Once a month, perhaps. Whatever was on his mind. He'd read the letters aloud to me—at age eleven, a captive audience. They all began the same way: "My Dearest, Darling Mr. President—Don't you listen to them when they say you can't do such-and-such and so-and-so...." Even when he *didn't* agree with his president—it was still the same salutation: "My Dearest, Darling Mr. President—You had no business to say so-and-so and such-and-such...."

We lived in a four-floor walk-up and so I, of course, ran down each day for the mail. And there, every once in a while, in my grandfather's mailbox, 74 York Street, New Haven, Connecticut—there would be that familiar little white envelope marked "The White House." Where else but in America? It awed me—and made me an inveterate letter-writer to my representatives.

I cannot overstate what being a citizen means to me. Felix Frankfurter said that the highest office in a democracy is the office of citizen. I believe that with all my heart. This government, which functions through the "consent of the governed," is *our* government. And the Congress and the president, who work for us, on our payroll, are *our* Congress and president. When we feel that strongly enough, we lose no opportunity to exercise our right—our obligation—to affect the decisions of our government.

In a democracy, the will of the majority rules—as it should. But at the same time, the conscience and the rights of the individual are sacred, and *also* deserve protection. So the Founding Fathers came up with one of the greatest inventions of modern statecraft: an independent judiciary. Without the federal courts, our constitutional rights could evaporate overnight. An irresponsible majority, hell-bent to punish its enemies, could suddenly decide to suspend freedom of speech or freedom of religion. Need I add that the first victims of a self-righteous majority would be ethnic and religious groups and individuals who happen to be unpopular? Scapegoats, sacrificed on the altar of freedom.

The Declaration of Independence laid forth the vision of a free society. The Constitution gave that vision structure. And the Bill of Rights enumerated and enshrined the most sacrosanct human rights. I cherish the First Amendment; to me, the words of the First Amendment are absolute: "Congress shall make no law . . . " it says.

It doesn't say that there will be freedom of expression provided said expression does not run contrary to popular thought. It doesn't say that there will be freedom of expression provided said expressions have no tendency to subvert standing institutions. In the Soviet Union, there are vigorous debates over government policies—but no one is allowed to challenge the government itself, nor any activity of the government. How different is America with the blessing of the First Amendment.

America's founding documents affirm the spirit of liberty. What is the spirit of liberty? Judge Learned Hand once raised that question—and answered it.

I cannot define it. I can only tell you my own faith. The spirit of liberty is the spirit which seeks to understand the minds of other men and women; the spirit of liberty is a spirit which weighs their interests alongside its own without bias; the spirit of liberty remembers that not even one sparrow falls to earth unheeded; the spirit of liberty is the spirit of Him, who, near two thousand years ago, taught mankind a lesson it has never learned, but has never quite forgotten.

A new attack on the spirit of liberty was launched in 1980 with the merging of the political New Right with the growing "electronic church" of fundamentalist television evangelists—Jerry Falwell, Pat Robertson, Jimmy Swaggart, James Robison, Tim LaHaye, to name a few. The resulting Religious Right began to aggressively promote a radical proposition: That this nation is reserved for card-carrying Christians, and only *Fundamentalist* Christians at that.

Every generation must deal with its own infallibles. In the 1950s,

Joe McCarthy considered himself an infallible. To challenge his thinking or his methods was to be tagged immediately as being soft on communism. To disagree with the Religious Right's conclusions on numerous matters of morality and politics is to be labeled a poor Christian or unpatriotic or antifamily. They claimed to be a "Moral Majority," to speak with the "Christian Voice." John Buchanan, chairman of People for the American Way, has correctly described the Religious Right's tactics as "Moral McCarthyism."

Consider some of the statements these people have made:

- Jerry Falwell has said: "The idea that religion and politics don't mix was invented by the Devil to keep Christians from running their own country."

- Pat Robertson has said: "The Constitution of the United States is a marvelous document for self-government by Christian people. But the minute you turn the Constitution into the hands of non-Christian and atheistic people, they can use it to destroy the very foundation of our society. And that's what's been happening."

- Paul Weyrich has said: "We are talking about Christianizing America. We are talking about simply spreading the Gospel in a political context."

- And the Religious Right group, Christian Voice, has said: "In answer to your [People for the American Way's] silly attacks on us, there *is* only one godly position on issues like abortion, pornography, and homosexuality. That position is clearly stated in the Bible, which you are obviously unfamiliar with. How could *God* hold two positions on any issue?"

The leaders of the Religious Right have every First Amendment right to express themselves as they wish. That is both the pain and the glory of the First Amendment. But defending their right to speak out does not mean that what they say does not threaten the spirit of liberty—and it does not mean that we may not exercise our own First Amendment rights to protect constitutional values.

That is why I joined with leaders from the field of religion, education, business, and public policy to form People for the American Way in 1980. We are the only public interest organization which began as a sixty-second TV commercial, but we have grown from that original effort to an organization with more than 270,000 members.

We had two purposes in forming People for the American Way: the first was to provide a focused response to the Religious Right; the second was to defend and celebrate our constitutional liberties—and the spirit of liberty.

Our fight continues. When the media started picking Norman Lear out of People for the American Way and Jerry Falwell out of the Moral Majority and began butting our heads—we at People for the American Way begged them to understand that the problems presented by the Religious Right ran deep in the American body politic, and would only be trivialized by concentrating on a few symptoms, namely the TV evangelists.

We tried to help them see that there was more going on:

- The effort to remove books like *Huckleberry Finn, The Grapes of Wrath,* and *The Diary of Anne Frank* from libraries and classrooms in most of the fifty states.

- The effort to censor textbooks and curricula and to spread the myth that the religion of "secular humanism" was transforming American institutions.

- The constant attack on public education.

- The call for a constitutional convention, ostensibly to get a balanced budget amendment, but more subtly aimed at rewriting the First and Fourteenth Amendments.

- The effort to subvert the independent judiciary by appointing only judges who pass an ideological litmus test.

- The effort to take over local school boards and political party structures.

All of these efforts threaten America's constitutional liberties. Yet, ironically, we owe the Religious Right a debt of gratitude. When the Religious Right speaks to the need for pride in our country, standards for our lives, and nourishment for our spirits, they are addressing the right problems. When they talk of failures in our educational system, the erosion of our moral standards, and the waste of young lives, they are addressing real and legitimate concerns.

But when they ignore the constitutionally mandated separation of church and state and make their sectarian dogma the standard for political and social life—when they tell us that putting prayer back in the public schools will solve the problems of teenage suicide and drug use—they are misleading millions of us, blurring our vision of the real problems and causing great damage.

Of all the falsehoods and confusions and misunderstandings for which they are responsible, this one angers me the most: that the division in our society is between those who have absolute, unquestioned biblically mandated values—and the rest of us, who supposedly have no values at all.

The fact is, the majority of Americans *do* share a core of values about right and wrong, the virtuous life, and the common good, even while respecting each other's rights to think, worship, and vote in different ways. Most Protestants, Catholics, Jews, Muslims, and even "secular humanists" share a set of beliefs on how we should live here on Earth, even as we differ over questions that may never be settled in this life. Republicans, Democrats, and Independents share a commitment to democracy and the rule of law, even as they debate the myriad ways to execute that commitment.

The Religious Right's claim that America's choice is between its own "biblical" values and no values at all has poisoned the debate about the relationship of church and state, of religion and politics, in our nation. The Religious Right myth holds that if its values are not codified, then all values and all religion have been driven out of the public arena. That is a lie. America is a nation built on a moral covenant with its people—an America which banished values from public debate would be unimaginable.

We at People for the American Way remain committed to our original goals—to respond to the Religious Right and to offer a positive vision of America's values. That commitment includes showing Americans that while the Religious Right offers the wrong way to "mix religion and politics," there is a right and proper way to do so, while respecting our national heritage and the spirit of liberty.

Acknowledgments

I have been following the intricate relationship between religion and politics as a journalist since 1972, when it became clear that Richard Nixon and George McGovern were waging a holy war as much as a political campaign. Since 1985, I have addressed the issue in more detail through my work with People for the American Way, a non-partisan constitutional liberties organization founded in 1980 to counter the influence of the Religious Right and to defend American constitutional values.

Most recent books written on the subject of religion and politics have tended to offer either theory and history without a firm grounding in recent events, or more limited attacks on the Religious Right. This books is an effort to present both a framework within which to understand the relationship between religion and politics, and concrete illustrations of the many and varied ways in which the two interact on a daily basis.

Several individuals associated with People for the American Way deserve mention for their help in preparing this book. Chapter 5, on the 1986 elections, is based primarily on material collected under the direction of Carol Keys in the library and Tina Hester in the field office. Chapter 6, on Pat Robertson, is based in large part on his "700 Club" appearances transcribed over the years by Cindy Gibson, Naomi Levan, and Deborah Russell. David Kusnet and Melanne Verveer helped refine some of the arguments in key chapters. I would also like to thank Norman Lear, John Buchanan, Tony Podesta, Art Kropp, Chuck Bergstrom, and David Crane for their support in this project. Final responsibility for judgments and conclusions, however, rests with the author.

Jim Castelli

1. How to Mix Religion and Politics

Few issues in America today generate as much heat and as little light as "mixing religion and politics." Discussion of the issue is inflamed by the fact that it is the object of several passionately held, though often conflicting, myths:

- *The Religious Right Myth of a Golden Age*: According to this view, the United States was founded as a Christian nation, but turned its back on God by throwing Him out of the public schools, legalizing abortion, and following the new religion of "secular humanism"; the only way to save the nation's soul is to Christianize it through its electoral politics, courts, and public schools.

- *The Neo-Conservative Myth of the Naked Public Square*: Best explained by Lutheran pastor Richard John Neuhaus, this is a somewhat more respectable version of the Myth of a Golden Age. Neuhaus argues that liberal politics and the Supreme Court have banished traditional religion from the public sphere, creating a "naked public square," which is then filled by "an ersatz religion," a worship of the state.

- *The Liberal Myth of Purely Private Religion*: In this view, religious freedom is seen as the right of all Americans to practice the faith of their choice in private, while keeping their religion out of public debate.

- *The Myth of the Secular City*: In 1965, Harvard theologian Harvey Cox saw a world in which religious influence was declining and declared it a good thing; he heralded the arrival of a "secular city," in which religion played a less influential role and the positive values of secularism dominated. In 1984, Cox wrote *Religion in the Secular City*, in which he claimed to discover a "reappearance" of religion in the secular city.

- *The Media Myth of Impotent/Omnipotent Religion*: This myth is not stated directly, but can be inferred from media coverage of religion; the media alternate between largely ignoring the role of religion in human, particularly political, affairs, and acting as though a Jerry Falwell or the Catholic bishops have the power singlehandedly to change the outcome of elections.

The debate over the relationship of religion and politics is also subject to simplistic sloganeering: "Don't mix religion and politics"; "We are a Christian nation"; "A strict wall of separation between church and state."

Actually, it's unfair to describe the "wall of separation of church and state" as a slogan because it is a phrase with a long, distinguished history. It is, however, often used as a slogan meant to end discussion, not advance it. This problem illustrates yet another source of confusion—disagreement over the meaning of terms like "church," "state," "religion," "politics," and "society."

For example, a person who supports a "wall of separation" may mean that the US Constitution forbids the state from dictating religious beliefs—and, of course, this would be right. But another person hearing about a "wall of separation" might interpret that to mean that religious and moral beliefs have no basis in the public arena; this person would argue that that's not what the Constitution means, and, of course, this too would be right.

Several tasks face us if we are to improve the ratio of light to heat in the American "religion-and-politics" debate: We must define terms more precisely, explode the myths shaping the debate, create a framework for approaching the relationship of religion and politics, and develop some rules for mixing religion and politics.

Above all, in sorting out the tangled relationship between religion and politics, we must use common sense. "Common sense" has been an integral part of the American psyche since Tom Paine wrote a pamphlet of that name to encourage the American revolution and advance the ideas which became the basis for the Declaration of Independence. While *Common Sense* did not address the relationship between religion and politics, the concept is essential in untangling that relationship today.

The easiest task is clarifying the terms used in the debate. A considerable amount of confusion and anger stem from the identification of the state with the society. The "state" refers to the government; "society" refers to the entire social body, which includes the state, individuals, and mediating institutions such as churches, unions, neighborhood organizations, and other voluntary associations. A nation in which the "state" and "society" are identical is totalitarian—and totalitarianism may be atheistic or theistic in nature, the Soviet Union or Islamic Iran. Anyone who fails to understand the distinction between state and society is threatened by the notion of keeping specifically religious symbols and beliefs out of the activities of the "state"; such a course of action appears to delegitimize the role of religion. But understanding the difference between "state" and "society" allows for a legitimate role for religion—including as a force interacting with the state.

Just as it is essential to distinguish "state" from "society," it is also essential to distinguish "church" from "religion": "church" refers to official institutions of believers, not the believers themselves acting as individuals; "religion" refers to a value system—members of a church do not necessarily practice a religion, and those who do not belong to a church may still profess a religious worldview.

Politics, like religion, is a process, an activity through which various elements within a society debate values and goals and form policies to guide the state. This kind of politics does not exist in a totalitarian society—or a theocracy. The separation of church and state, then, is not the same thing as the separation of religion and politics. Church and state, as institutions, must be kept separate; religion and politics, as processes of thought and action, cannot be kept separate.

While church-state and religion-and-politics issues obviously overlap, they are still essentially different. A focus on church-state issues generally involves detailed discussion of Supreme Court rulings on interactions between government and religious institutions on questions of parochial school aid, public displays of religious symbols, school prayer, and so on. Much of that discussion is useful, but it can become too narrow in focus. William Lee Miller, in *The First Liberty: Religion and the American Republic* (1985), offers a marvelous piece of satire on a hypothetical church-state case involving a minister who places a Bible verse on a municipal water fountain used by a city soft-ball league. The ensuing legal arguments call to mind a "Herman" cartoon featuring a man holding a very long leash at the end of which is a very small dog. "He's not housetrained," the man says, "but who cares?"; the sign on the water fountain may be unconstitutional, but who cares?

To focus on religion and politics, on the other hand, is to focus on the behavior of religious people and institutions, politicians, and all those concerned with the moral dimension of public policy. The is-sues are larger, the players generally better known, and the impact on public debate more substantial.

The most common misconception in the religion and politics de-bate is that "religion" and "values" are identical entities. For some people, this is a misconception; for the Religious Right, it is an arti-cle of faith and ideology. Some of the confusion stems from the words of our first president. George Washington said in his farewell address that "religion and morality are indispensable supports" for political prosperity and that "reason and experience both forbid us to expect that national morality can prevail in exclusion of religious principle."

Whatever the case in Washington's day, however, "reason and ex-perience" today show that it is possible to have morality in the ab-sence of religious beliefs just as it is possible to hold religious beliefs in the absence of morality. William Lee Miller makes this point well:

Today, as yesterday, it is by no means clear that "Religion" (undifferentiated and capitalized) can by itself provide the full foundation of republican gov-ernment. "Religion" comes in many varieties. Among other results, it pro-duces indifference on the one side, and fanaticism on the other side, of public life. It has sanctified many cruelties.

Patrick Henry and Timothy Dwight and the broad American public of the 19th Century, and the conservative religionists and presidents of the 20th, are surely wrong when they assert—without inquiring any further—that "Religion" will provide the Republic's requisite "morality." It may or may not. The same, of course, is true of "secularism." So there needs to be an interplay.

Social science also shows that religion and ethical values are not identical. For example, Gallup Organization surveys show that Americans rank ahead of most Western European nations in church attendance, belief in a personal God, and the importance of God in their lives; but the United States also ranks ahead of those same nations in teenage pregnancy and abortion rates and has the highest percentage of drug users in the industrialized world. At the same time, George Gallup, Jr., reports that although there has been a moderate religious revival in the United States in the 1980s, there has been no corresponding increase in ethical behavior.

Social scientists also see a difference between "morality" and "religion" at the practical level. Larry Nucci of the University of Illinois at Chicago has done some research which sheds light on this distinction. Nucci and his associates interviewed about three hundred Catholic, Jewish, Amish, and conservative Mennonite children to see if they saw distinctions between acts which were wrong because they violated some rules—whether school or religious—and acts which were wrong because of their very nature. They found children as young as three made such distinctions.

For example, Nucci cited a conversation with a three-year-old girl about two activities at preschool. In one instance, she told an interviewer that some children had been noisy and that there was a rule that said they were supposed to be quiet. If there were no rule, she said, it would be all right to be noisy.

But her reaction was different when she saw two boys playing and one hit the other:

Q: Did you see what just happened?
A: Yes. They were playing and John hit him too hard.
Q: Is that something you are supposed to or not supposed to do?
A: Not so hard to hurt.
Q: Is there a rule about that?
A: Yes.

Q: What is the rule?

A: You're not to hit hard.

Q: What if there were no rule about hitting hard, would it be right to do then?

A: No.

Q: Why not?

A: Because he could get hurt and start to cry.

Nucci concluded that "1) children's moral understandings are independent of specific religious rules; 2) morality is conceptually distinct from one's religious concepts; and 3) morality for the secular child, as well as for the devout Jew or Christian, focuses on the same set of fundamental interpersonal issues: those pertaining to justice and compassion."

Arguing that morality and religion are not identical is neither a putdown of religion nor an attempt to banish religion from the public sphere. It merely allows us to talk about the values of the society— civic values— without either accepting or rejecting specific religious values.

RELIGION, POLITICS, AND THE FOUNDERS

As we try to make sense of the religion and politics debate today, we would do well to look at where we have been as a nation. From the earliest colonial days, two warring religious themes have dominated American life—religious intolerance and religious idealism. Contemporary Americans cannot be guided completely by the nation's Founders for the simple reason that we live in a world they could never have imagined. But we must be aware of the world in which they did live and the way it shaped their views on matters which affect our lives today.

The easiest myth about the nation's founding to set straight is the Christian Right claim that the United States was founded as a Christian nation. Biblical theology did have an influence on the Founders, but not in such a way that it is possible, as some imply, to deduce the Constitution from the New Testament. There were two other major sources of influence on the Founders: the Enlightenment philosophy of government as social contract, and the classical republican theories of the Greeks and Romans. The Rev. William F. Schulz, president of the Unitarian Universalist Association, notes that it is no more necessary to have a Christian nation to honor the influence of theology than it is to worship Zeus or Athena to honor the influence of the Greeks and Romans.

Three contemporary Evangelical historians—Mark Noll, Nathan Hatch, and George Marsden—put the issue in context in their book, *The Search for Christian America* (1983). The American Revolution, they tell us, "was not Christian, but it stood for many things compatible with the Christian faith. It was not biblical, though many of its founders respected Scripture. It did not establish the United States on a Christian foundation, even if it created many commendable precedents."

Noll, Hatch, and Marsden point out that

the Declaration of Independence . . . is based on an appeal to "self-evident" truths or "laws of nature and nature's God." The reference to God is vague and subordinated to natural laws that everyone should know through common sense. The Bible is not mentioned or alluded to. The Constitution of 1787 says even less concerning a deity, let alone Christianity or the Bible. [The United States] was the first western nation to omit explicitly religious symbolism, such as the cross, from its flag and other early national symbols.

At another level, Noll, Hatch, and Marsden point out that in terms of behavior—toward slaves, Indians, women, immigrants, and so on—the United States has never been a "Christian nation."

Historian Henry Steele Commager notes in a 1983 *Free Inquiry* article that in a 1796 treaty with Tripoli, President George Washington said that his country had no problem dealing with a Muslim country because "the government of the United States is not, in any sense, founded on the Christian religion."

Technically, the United States is a secular nation in the sense that it is not a sectarian one. But in crafting a secular nation, the Founders were under no illusion that Americans were a secular people. They appreciated and understood the importance of religion in their own lives, in the lives of their countrymen—and in the life of the new republic.

Several major factors influenced the Founders' views on the relationship of church and state, religion and politics. One was the simple fact of religious pluralism. The collection of Anglicans, Baptists, Catholics, Congregationalists, Jews, Lutherans, Methodists, Presbyterians, Quakers, Unitarians, and members of countless other denominations present in the Colonies was unmatched anywhere in the world. There was no way to fashion a new nation which gave official preference to one denomination over the others without insuring that the nation would not soon be torn apart. The Founders also came to see that pluralism was more than passive tolerance of diversity; it was a positive element which placed value on the contributions different groups made to the whole society.

A second influence on the Founders was distrust of established churches. Early colonial history had provided ample evidence of the persistence of religious intolerance. The history of the Virginia Statute for Establishing Religious Freedom illustrates this concern about religious intolerance. That statute, drafted by Thomas Jefferson and shepherded through the legislature by James Madison, provided much of the intellectual base for the separation of church and state found in the First Amendment to the US Constitution. Jefferson regarded the Virginia Statute as one of his three greatest accomplishments and the fight for religious liberty as "the severest contest in which I have ever been engaged."

Many of the original colonies had established state religions, but Virginia's case was particularly dramatic. Anglicanism was the established religion, but because it was so closely associated with the English, it had little popular support. "Dissenting" churches—Baptists, Presbyterians, Lutherans, German Pietists, and liberal churchmen like Jefferson and Madison—launched a series of attacks on the church establishment, including a section written by Madison and George Mason for the new state constitution granting all citizens "the free exercise of religion." The state legislature officially disestablished religion in 1779, ending its financial support for Anglican institutions.

But Jefferson was still not satisfied. Others, including George Washington, were content to have all Christian churches equally established; but he wanted absolute religious freedom and equality.

While Jefferson was in Paris, Madison, George Mason, and others successfully introduced the Statute for Establishing Religious Freedom, which passed by a 67 to 20 vote on December 17, 1885, and took effect a month later.

The statute began by acknowledging the existence of an all-powerful God—a God powerful and secure enough to allow rights for all, even nonbelievers:

Well aware that Almighty God hath created the mind free; that all attempts to influence it by temporal punishments or burdens, or by civil incapacitations, tend only to beget habits of hypocrisy and meanness, and are a departure from the plans of the Holy Author of our religion, who being Lord both of body and mind, yet chose not to propagate it by coercion on either, as was in his Almighty power to do.

Jefferson wrote in his autobiography that an effort to have the statute read ". . . Jesus Christ, the Holy Author of our religion . . ." was soundly defeated by the legislature, proving that "they meant to comprehend, within the mantle of its protection, the Jew and the Gentile, the Christian and the Mohammedan, the Hindu, the Infidel of every denomination."

The statute complained about "the impious presumptions of legislators and rulers . . . who . . . have assumed dominion over the faith of others, setting up their own opinions and modes of thinking as the only true and infallible."

Addressing the question of state financial support for religion, the statute said that "to compel a man to furnish contributions of money for the propagation of opinions which he disbelieves is sinful and tyrannical." It said state support for religion "tends also to corrupt the principles of that very religion it is meant to encourage, by bribing, with a monopoly of worldly honors and emoluments, those who will externally profess and conform to it."

The statute set forth a principle that guided the Founders as they drafted the Constitution: "Our civil rights have no dependence on our religious opinions, more than on our opinions in physics or geometry." The heart of the Virginia Statute is found in its enactment paragraph:

We, the General Assembly, do enact, that no man shall be compelled to frequent or support any religious worship, place or ministry whatsoever, nor shall be enforced, restrained, molested, or burdened in his body or goods, nor shall otherwise suffer on account of his religious opinions or belief; but that all men shall be free to possess and by argument maintain their opinions in matters of religion, and that the same shall in no wise diminish, enlarge or effect their civil capacities.

The history of the Virginia Statute contains an element which is ironic, given the terms of the contemporary debate over the relationship of religion and politics. Legislators do not pass laws in a vacuum, and the context of the birth of the Virginia Statute included a political coalition that does not seem possible today: Deists like Jefferson and Madison, who would probably be branded as "secular humanists" today, and the large numbers of Evangelical Christians in Virginia. William Lee Miller points out that, "For the American system of religious liberty, as for the American system of government, Jefferson, Madison and a small group of other heirs of the Enlightenment furnished much of the brainpower, but the religion of revival furnished the troops."

The need for religious liberty was not the only issue linking the Deists and the Evangelicals. While the Founders were convinced that there should be no established national religion and that religious intolerance was a serious danger, they were also influenced by certain beliefs that had their origin in religion, but were shared by believer and nonbeliever alike.

The first was the belief that religious liberty was good for religion itself. Miller and A. James Reichley, in *Religion in American Public Life* (1985), make this point. They give due credit to the influence of Roger Williams, the seventeenth-century Baptist reformer and religious liberty advocate, who argued that "The civil sword may make a nation of hypocrites and anti-Christians, but not one true Christian."

Religious beliefs also shaped early American attitudes toward government. In *A Religious History of the American People* (1972), Sydney Ahlstrom wrote that "Puritanism provided the moral and religious background of fully 75 percent of the people who declared their independence in 1776." The Puritans' faith, which included a strong emphasis on personal piety, found its political expression in support for individual human rights and the rule of law; Ahlstrom says the Puritans "recognized that governments, constitutions and laws were instituted to restrain man's sin and hence were truly of God."

Reichley quotes the nineteenth-century historian James Bryce, who said, "There is a hearty Puritanism in the view of human nature that pervades the instrument of 1787. It is the work of men who believed in original sin, and were resolved to leave open for transgressors no door which they could possibly shut." Reichley says it was this sense of original sin that led the Founders to devise a system of checks and balances within the new government to prevent any one branch—executive, Congress, or courts— from abusing power.

Finally, the Founders shared the belief that religion supported the common good. While they did not want an official religion, they were convinced that religion made an important contribution to society by supporting a sense of personal responsibility and a commitment to the common good.

Henry Steele Commager notes that, "A common religion did flourish among the Protestants, Catholics, Jews and Deists. We have come to call that a civil religion." Commager says that civil religion

relied on reason as well as faith, embraced mankind, rather than the individual, and was ever conscious of the claims of posterity. . . . It did not reject Jesus or the Gospels, but took from them what was universally valid. Its testaments, moral, philosophical, or political, celebrated virtue, happiness, equality in the sight of God and the law and life here rather than hereafter.

In *Habits of the Heart* (1985), sociologist Robert Bellah, who made popular the term "civil religion," says that for America's Founders, the political function of religion "was not direct intervention, but support of the mores that made democracy possible. In particular, it had the role of placing limits on utilitarian individualism, hedging in self-interest with a proper concern for others."

Historian Martin Marty examines the "civil religion" further in *Pilgrims in Their Own Land: 500 Years of Religion in America* (1984). Marty argues that Abraham Lincoln picked up on a tradition which Benjamin Franklin described as the "public religion"; Lincoln called it the "political religion." Marty writes,

As Franklin through his writings assumed such a faith [public religion] could draw on the points of agreement or of overlap in the religion of the churches, or what Franklin called "the essentials of every religion." These essentials, each sect would insist, were not to be used to save souls or make sad hearts glad, but they did assist the society in its search for some sort of moral consensus to support public order. This public faith—or as Lincoln would have it, this political religion—also helped form private character—which was an element in the proposal of Franklin—and clearly it helped steel the president for the crisis of war.

In recent years, Pat Robertson and other Religious Right leaders have claimed that the phrase "separation of church and state" does not appear in the US Constitution and does, in fact, appear in the Soviet Constitution. The words "separation of church and state" may not appear in the US Constitution, but the concept certainly does. Article VI says, "No religious test shall ever be required as a qualification to any office or public trust under the United States." This is a clear stand against religious intolerance and an affirmation that, in the spirit of the Virginia Statute, no American's religious beliefs should have an impact on his or her standing in the community.

In a pamphlet, *No Religious Test: The Story of Our Constitution's Forgotten Article* (1987), Albert J. Menendez of Americans United for Separation of Church and State describes the background of Article VI. "The world of 1787 was a grim place, as far as religious liberty was concerned," Menendez wrote. "Every nation had an established religion with little or no legal protection for religious dissenters or minorities. These establishment states accorded first-class citizenship only to members of the preferred religious group. No dissenter need apply."

At the time of the American Revolution, Menendez noted, nine of the thirteen colonies had established state religions. Even those which did not limited public office to Protestants, although Catholics and Jews were occasionally elected to office despite those laws. When the Constitutional Convention met, Charles Pinckney, a delegate from South Carolina—and a member of the state's established Episcopal church—proposed the ban on a religious test for office under the new federal government. Such a ban, he said, was "a provision the world will expect from you in the establishment of a system founded on republican principles and in an age so liberal and enlightened as the present."

"While Pinckney's optimism seems a bit naive in retrospect," Menendez wrote, "he judged the opinions of his fellow delegates accurately. . . . Some records suggest a unanimous vote in favor of the ban on religious tests."

Menendez notes that a prominent supporter of the ban on a religious test for office was Oliver Ellsworth, who was Chief Justice of the US Supreme Court from 1796 to 1800. Ellsworth noted that some people were concerned that the article was hostile to religion. But Ellsworth said,

The sole purpose and effect of it is to exclude persecution and to secure the important right of religious liberty. . . . A test-law is the parent of hypocrisy and the offspring of error and the spirit of persecution. Legislatures have no right to set up an inquisition, and examine into the private opinions of men. Test-laws are useless and ineffectual, unjust and tyrannical; therefore Convention have done wisely in excluding this engine of persecution in providing that no religious test shall ever be required.

When the First Congress agreed that a Bill of Rights was needed to clarify the Constitution, religious liberty was one of its priority issues. The First Amendment declares that "Congress shall make no law respecting an establishment of religion, or prohibiting the free exercise thereof." These sixteen words have generated virtually unlimited controversy.

But several things about the First Amendment are clear. It barred the establishment of a national religion and guaranteed US citizens freedom of religion. It did not prohibit the individual states from having established religions; several states did, in fact, continue to have established churches after the ratification of the Bill of Rights. But, those establishments were dying, and the last established church, in Massachusetts, was gone by 1833. In a sense, it was not necessary to bar state religions, because history demanded that they disappear.

In trying to understand what the Founders wanted to do in terms of the relationship between church and state and religion and politics, it is necessary to remember that the Constitution is, in the best sense of the word, a political document: it reflects compromises of the time and was designed to bind a new society together—and to keep it together. This means that the Constitution, as originally ratified, did not resolve all aspects of the church-state, religion-politics issues any more than it resolved all aspects of civil rights—the Constitution did, after all, accept the existence of slavery, and voting rights for male landowners only.

Justice Thurgood Marshall notes that the Constitution was "defective from the start, requiring several amendments, a civil war, and momentous social transformations to attain the system of constitutional government, and its respect for the individual freedoms and human rights, we hold as fundamental today." One of the changes Marshall had in mind was basic: it took the Fourteenth Amendment and later court interpretation of it to apply the Bill of Rights—including the First Amendment—to the states.

The Founders intended the Constitution as a document which would contain fixed principles, yet allow for structural changes and refinements as the new nation grew; the very fact that the First Congress attached the Bill of Rights to the Constitution illustrates this. American sensitivity to civil rights has grown over the past two centuries; we have seen the end of slavery, the universal vote, the women's and civil rights movements. We have reached a sense of balance concerning what the states and the federal government, respectively, may regulate. We have seen that it is intolerable for a state to be able to limit a basic right which is guaranteed to the citizens of the nation.

Sensitivity to the meaning of the religious liberty that was so important to the Founders has also grown as we have come to understand better the implications of a secular government for a religious people. It isn't necessary to agree with every Supreme Court decision on these issues—and the court itself offers a shifting majority with each case—to concede that the movement has been toward a greater guarantee of religious liberty.

RELIGION, POLITICS, AND U.S. HISTORY

Many discussions of the relationship between religion and politics leapfrog from the constitutional era to the present, but this approach ignores a great deal of American history. Without claiming to offer a detailed history, the following survey gives an indication of the role religion has played in American history—for both good and ill:

- The "Great Awakening" of the mid-eighteenth century was a wave of Evangelical Christianity with an emphasis on personal conversion and spirituality which helped democratize American institutions.

- Colonial preachers like Jonathan Mayhew of Boston used the Bible as the basis for sermons promoting liberty during the prerevolutionary and revolutionary period, stirring up passions and earning the label from the British of "The Black Regiment" for their support of the war effort.

- The churches led the way in establishing the Indian territories and, later, in civilizing the frontier as the population moved westward.

- Religious leaders led the movement to make dueling illegal in the wake of the death of Alexander Hamilton in a duel with Aaron Burr.

- Religious leaders came together to form the common schools to educate children when no one church was strong enough in a frontier area to form its own school.

- Protestant and Quaker leaders led the abolition movement to free America's slaves, and religion played a central role in the lives of southern blacks before and after the Civil War.

- The "Know-Nothing" movement of Protestant nativists created a wave of discrimination against new Catholic immigrants in the mid-nineteenth century.

- Religion played a major role in maintaining communities of new immigrants and socializing them into the American system.

- Religious leaders helped launch the Women's Suffrage movement.
- Churches established a whole network of independent hospitals, schools, orphanages, and charitable services.
- The social encyclicals of Pope Leo XIII and the support of James Cardinal Gibbons of Baltimore for the rights of labor helped preserve the labor movement in the United States.
- Baptist and Methodist churches led the temperance movement, which culminated in Prohibition.

Religion continued to play a prominent role in American society even after Harvey Cox discovered the "secular city":

- In the mid-1960s, the Civil Rights movement, and the Anti-Vietnam War movement, were both led by clergymen and others citing religious, moral, and ethical reasons for their support for civil rights and opposition to the war.
- In his 1968 and 1972 campaigns, Richard Nixon pursued a "Southern strategy" that was aimed at attracting support from traditionally Democratic southern Evangelicals; for years it was almost impossible to go to the White House without tripping over Billy Graham.
- When Nixon's career took a downward twist, the term "Watergate morality" entered the vocabulary and provided the force behind Democratic congressional gains in 1974 and 1976 as well as the election of Jimmy Carter, a self-professed "born-again Christian," as president in 1976.
- The abortion issue, which has been heating up since the mid-1960s, is nothing if not a religious issue, with both sides citing moral and religious arguments.
- The emergence of the Religious Right in the 1980s has influenced the shape of the political debate in America.
- In the 1980s, religious leaders, particularly the US Catholic bishops, have been in the forefront of opposition to US policy in Central America and in support of arms control negotiations and agreements.

Even a cursory survey of the role of religion in American history shows that the city isn't secular and the public square isn't naked.

The harshest critics of contemporary society's treatment of religion usually point to a few issues on which they were on the losing side as proof that religion has been driven from public life; but these examples do not prove their case. For example, the Supreme Court decisions barring government-written-and-sponsored prayer in the public schools has been a rallying point for the Religious Right, but mainline religious leaders have long opposed government-sponsored school prayer, partly on the grounds that it trivializes religion. Martin Marty notes, in an essay in *Religion in American Public Life* (1986), that

public school rites had largely disappeared before the Supreme Court acted against devotions in 1962 and 1963. Administrators, when polled, reported that in exactly 99.44 percent of their districts moral values were taught, but only 6.4 percent of the Midwest schools and 2.4 percent of the West Coast ones knew anything like homeroom devotional practices. The people ritually "took God out of the schools" before the Supreme Court did.

Others point to the Supreme Court's decisions on abortion as a negative turning point. But while Catholics and Evangelicals have been in the forefront of those urging strict laws against abortion, mainline Protestant and Jewish religious leaders have been in the forefront of those urging permissive abortion laws. The fact is that abortion is an issue on which the religious community is divided; no matter what side the Supreme Court came down on, it would have been accused of violating religious freedom.

At the same time, the aftermath of the Court's decisions shows that although the court made abortion legal, it did not remove it as a moral issue in the public sphere: it is still hotly debated and, most likely, always will be; abortion opponents have succeeded in ending federal funding for abortion and many states bar abortion funding; there are programs, including some with government support, which emphasize providing social services for women with problem pregnancies who opt not to have abortions.

Presidential elections for the past quarter-century have also consistently focused on values; again, the losers in a given election have often felt that their loss meant that all values had been pushed aside, but that has not been the case. In 1960, religious intolerance was an issue as Americans elected their first Catholic president. In 1964, the issue was the rejection of extremism in the Goldwater campaign. In 1968, the issues were peace and "law and order." In 1972, President Nixon replayed his law-and-order campaign, while George McGovern urged, "Come Home, America," in a call for repentance for the national sin of war.

In 1976, Gerald Ford, who succeeded to the presidency when Nixon resigned in the wake of the Watergate scandal, ran on the basis that he had restored trust in government; Jimmy Carter called for an emphasis on human rights in foreign policy and pledged to give the nation "a government as good as its people." In 1980, Ronald Reagan challenged claims of a national "malaise." In 1984, Walter Mondale spoke of compassion while Reagan spoke of national pride.

The nation saw a revival of "Watergate Morality" in the wake of the Reagan administration's secret arms sales to the Iranian terrorists in the hopes of releasing American hostages and the diversion of resulting funds to the Nicaraguan Contras. The scandal destroyed the administration's credibility overnight as Americans responded to a basic moral belief—they want their government to tell the truth and obey the law.

COMMON SENSE AND CIVIL RELIGION

The preceding pages have moved us toward a clearer understanding of the relationship between religion and politics in America. First, we clarified the terms of the debate to show that the "separation of church and state" does not require the separation of religion and politics. Then, we exploded the major myths affecting the debate: we saw that the United States was not created as a Christian nation; we also saw that the nation's Founders never intended religion to be relegated to the private sphere; we saw that religion has been an influence throughout American history; and we saw that there is no naked public square or secular city.

What we need now is a common sense framework within which to approach the mixing of religion and politics. We can find the basis for that framework in the ideas of the Founders. The framework is a belief in the concept of civil religion—in two senses.

First, there is a civil religion in the sense that American citizens share common values, the values that Benjamin Franklin, Abraham Lincoln, and others referred to when they spoke of public religion: the values of the Constitution and the Declaration of Independence—justice, equality, freedom, democracy, tolerance, compassion, concern for the general welfare, self-reliance, hard work, respect. Emlynn I. Griffith, regent of the University of the State of New York, in a 1987 address to the National School Boards Association, pointed out that as Alexis de Tocqueville observed 150 years ago, they are the "shared values which 'hold together' a very diverse nation."

"These civic virtues," Griffith said,

can be distinguished from religious values, which usually concentrate on the supernatural or mystical (and should not be taught in public schools for First Amendment reasons). Basic values and theological values are different; learning the former does not mean automatic acceptance of the latter. But the fact that many civic values have roots in the Judeo-Christian tradition or in other world religions does not diminish their usefulness as legitimate standards of social conduct; and teaching them does not conflict with the First Amendment to our Constitution.

Civic values do not compete with religious values—they make no claims to ultimate authority. Civil religion makes no claim that its values will get you into heaven; it only claims that they will make you a good citizen.

Civil religion has at times appeared in a negative form—a kind of national idolatry in which American desires were identified with God's will. This is a distortion of civil religion, just as zealots have distorted other religions. Many of those on the Religious Right today use the language of religion to attack the most fundamental beliefs of the American civil religion.

A framework for approaching the mixing of religion and politics requires a second understanding of civil religion—the requirement that religious groups must practice civility in the public arena. The Religious Right rejects civility as a sign of lack of commitment to "biblical" values, but the Founders rightly saw that civility was essential to the maintenance of the republic. The best contemporary advice in this regard comes from Joseph Cardinal Bernardin of Chicago, who put it this way: "We should maintain and clearly articulate our religious convictions, but also maintain our civil courtesy. We should be vigorous in stating a case and attentive in hearing another's case; we should test everyone's logic, but not question his or her motives."

FIVE RULES FOR MIXING RELIGION AND POLITICS

Much of the debate over the relationship of religion and politics involves wasted effort on the question of *whether* to mix religion and politics. But it is inevitable that the two will be mixed; the more fruitful discussion should revolve around the question of *how* to mix religion and politics. The framework we have established suggests the following rules for mixing religion and politics:

1. It is legitimate to discuss the moral dimension of public issues.

This should be obvious, but some critics of the Religious Right have overreacted and tried to push discussions of morality out of the public debate altogether; they are joined by many Kissingeresque "realists" who want to dismiss morality as irrelevant in foreign affairs. But American political debate would be unrecognizable without moral argument; the Founders clearly understood this. Columnist George Will, in a 1983 interview with *Our Sunday Visitor,* asserted, "American politics is currently afflicted by kinds of grim, moralizing groups that are coarse in their conceptions, vulgar in analysis and intemperate in advocacy. But the desirable alternative to such groups is not less preoccupation with this sort of question, but better preoccupation. . . . Absent good moral argument, bad moral argument will have the field to itself."

In *Religion in American Public Life* (1985), A. James Reichley offered a sound assessment of the role the churches play in public debate:

From the standpoint of the public good, the most important service churches offer to secular life in a free society is to nurture moral values that help humanize capitalism and give direction to democracy. Up to a point, participation by the churches in the formulation of public policy, particularly on issues with clear moral content, probably strengthens their ability to perform this nurturing function. If the churches were to remain silent on issues like civil rights or nuclear war or abortion, they would soon lose moral credibility. But if the churches become too involved in the hurly-burly of routine politics, they will eventually appear to their members and to the general public as special pleaders for ideological causes or even as appendages to transitory political factions. Each church must decide for itself where this point of political and moral peril comes. But it is in all our best interests that the churches not be frivolous in testing the limits of public tolerance.

2. In entering the political arena, religious leaders may not rely on doctrine, appeals to religious authority, or claims to speak for God to advance their case; they must play by the same rules as everyone else and argue their case on its merits.

This rule reflects the distinction between civil religion and sectarian religion. Civil religion deals with morality; while morality is a legitimate element of public debate, there is a crucial distinction between morality and doctrine. Morality is generic; Jews, Catholics, Baptists, Buddhists, and atheists can all agree that murder is a crime or debate the morality of foreign aid, for example, despite their religious differences. A religious doctrine, on the other hand, is acceptable only to those who share a particular faith and is not open to reasonable debate. Claims to speak for God or to hold the "biblical" position on an issue similarly violate this principle.

The distinction between morality and doctrine is explained well by David Little, professor of religion and sociology at the University of Virginia, in an essay in *Christianity and Politics,* published by The Ethics and Public Policy Center (1981). Describing the views of Roger Williams, the colonial Baptist known as the "father of American religious pluralism," Little discussed Williams's belief that "there existed an independent standard of public morality according to which governments might rightly be judged" and that "a commitment to religious pluralism must rest upon a shared belief that civil or public morality is determinable independent of religious beliefs."

Little notes that the Religious Right is inaccurate when it attempted to say it is merely doing what Martin Luther King, Jr., and other religious leaders supporting civil rights and opposing the Vietnam War did in their time. Little states that anti-Vietnam War religious leaders cited the "just war" theory, not doctrine. He pointed out,

Martin Luther King, Jr., made explicit and repeated appeals to the natural-law tradition, the American Constitution and the American heritage, which were combined with rather general references to the Christian tradition and to figures like Jesus and Gandhi. He did not advocate particular "Bible-based legislation" or threaten to defeat candidates who did not conform to an explicitly religious position.

Cardinal Bernardin of Chicago made the same crucial distinction in a 1983 address at Fordham University. In urging a "consistent ethic of life" that would link opposition to abortion to opposition to the use of nuclear weapons, capital punishment, social program budget cuts, and the reliance on military force in Central America, Bernardin said Catholics "face the challenge of stating our case, which is shaped in terms of our faith and our religious convictions, in nonreligious terms which others of different faith convictions might find morally persuasive."

This is the direct opposite of the approach taken by the Religious Right. To the Religious Right, there is no such thing as a "godly" person who is simply mistaken—if you disagree with them, you're in league with the devil. The result is the Satanization of American politics in which opponents become heretics and Democrats become infidels. This Satanization of American politics strikes at the very nature of civility and compromise on which the Constitution depends—God and Satan can't sit down and split the difference the way Robert Byrd and Robert Dole can.

The distinction between morality and doctrine makes it easy to see that while it may be arrogant to talk about forming a "Moral Majority," it is at least within the boundaries of pluralism, while the talk of forming a "Christian nation" is not. There are other examples:

• Federal courts have correctly held that "Scientific Creationism" should not be taught in the public schools because it required a belief in specific religious doctrine, a Fundamentalist interpretation of the Book of Genesis.

- It's unacceptable to base a Middle East policy on a particular interpretation of the Bible, such as the belief that because "Judea and Samaria" were part of Israel in the Bible, it is necessary to annex the West Bank today. Similarly, it's unacceptable to base unconditional support of Israel on a doctrinal belief about the necessity of a converted Israel to set the stage for the Second Coming of Christ.
- While there is sufficient religious basis for the obligation to feed the hungry and clothe the naked, a Bible verse alone is no more an acceptable justification for supporting a specific government program or a funding level than it is for opposing the Equal Rights Amendment.
- Belief in the biblical concept of "an eye for an eye" is not an acceptable basis for supporting capital punishment; belief that capital punishment is wrong because it precludes the opportunity for the convicted person's conversion is not an acceptable basis for opposing it.
- It's acceptable to use moral arguments for or against a bilateral US-Soviet nuclear freeze, but unacceptable to equate the freeze with godlessness or to condemn it on the basis that the Soviet Union is a "Satanic" power.

3. There can be no "religious test" for public office.

This rule comes straight from the Constitution itself. There is no religious test for office in the United States in the sense that the Founders specifically sought to bar a requirement that a candidate belong to a particular faith in order to be eligible for office. But there is a new form of religious test in America today that clearly violates the spirit of the Constitution—demands that candidates be "godly" or "probiblical" or "born-again Christians."

4. Government may not single out individuals or institutions for special treatment—favorable or unfavorable—on the basis of religion.

This is a simple restatement of the spirit of the Virginia Statute on Religious Liberty which Justice Sandra Day O'Connor restated well in a recent opinion:

The Establishment Clause prohibits government from making adherence to a religion in any way relevant to a person's standing in the political community. Government can run afoul of that prohibition in two principal ways. One is excessive entanglement with religious institutions. . . . The second and more direct infringement is government endorsements or disapproval of religion. Endorsement sends a message to nonadherents that they are outsiders, not full members of the political community, and an accompanying message to adherents that they are insiders, favored members of the political community. Disapproval sends the opposite message.

5. Public officials have every right to express their private piety, and no right at all to use their office to proselytize others.

To sum this up in the language of ecumenical dialogues, "Witness, yes; proselytization, no." Americans expect, and even like, a certain amount of piety in their public officials; referring to God can be a reassuring expression of humility, an expression of civil religion. Americans aren't threatened by a politician's private beliefs; non-Baptists weren't offended when Jimmy Carter taught at a Southern Baptist Sunday school while president. But it is improper for a public official—speaking officially—to ask people to believe in the Bible or to do something because it is commanded by "Our Lord, Jesus Christ"—as President Reagan has done.

These rules provide a useful basis for interpreting the many instances of the mixing of religion and politics in America in recent years and for assessing the future. In the following pages, we will examine the many and complex ways in which religion and politics are entwined in America today; we will see that the centuries-old American battle between religious intolerance and religious idealism is still alive; and we will see that Americans and their institutions are still struggling with the mixing of religion and politics.

2. Religion and Politics: Public Opinion and Behavior

Amidst all the controversy surrounding the debate over mixing religion and politics, there is little awareness of the degree to which religious belief and affiliation have an impact on American politics. The relationship is not simple; Americans do not vote for a candidate or support a bill because their religious leaders tell them to do so. But religious belief does influence political behavior in a variety of ways.

Social science findings on the relationship of religious belief and political belief are often contradictory. Dean Hoge, a sociologist at the Catholic University of America, has surveyed studies of what sociologists call "salience"—the degree to which a person's religious commitment predicts his political beliefs—and conducted a statistical analysis of a 1981 Gallup Poll in search of salience. He found little relationship between religious and political views. For example, religious commitment was in no way reliable as a predictor of attitudes toward money, work, free enterprise, prejudice, and intergroup relations or political activism. The only areas in which a direct relationship could be found was that the most religiously committed were more likely to value the church and to hold conservative attitudes on sexuality and family life, honesty and ethics in public life, and (for Protestants) alcohol.

On the other hand, a 1981 survey of American values conducted by Research & Forecasts Inc. for the Connecticut Mutual Life Insurance Company found that "it is the level of our religious commitment which, in the early part of the '80s, is a stronger determinant of our values than whether we are rich or poor, young or old, male or female, Black or White, liberal or conservative." The survey found:

- The most religious Americans are far more likely than the least religious to believe that the vote is the main thing that determines how the country is run (64 percent versus 32 percent).

- The most religious are much more likely to believe that important decisions on public issues are best left in the hands of our leaders (56 percent versus 36 percent).

- The most religious are more inclined to believe that major national problems can be solved through traditional American politics (41 percent versus 30 percent).

- The most religious Americans are distinctly more likely than the least religious to vote in local elections (77 percent versus 49 percent).

Another recent noteworthy study is reported in *Faith and Ferment: An Interdisciplinary Study of Christian Beliefs and Practices,* published jointly by Augsburg and Liturgical Presses. The book is based on an in-depth study of more than two thousand Christians in Minnesota. While the study found considerable diversity in attitudes about the church's involvement in political issues, Sister Joan Chittister, coauthor of the study, wrote, "it is startling to find three-quarters (76 percent) of the population certain that following Jesus implies taking the side of the poor and doing what is possible to secure systemic justice and to find almost half (43 percent) certain that liberation is an essential element of Christianity."

When it came to political involvement, "The concern was not whether or not Christian churches should be involved in public issues, but which issues ought to be the focus of the committed Christian," said Joan Chittister. "Two streams of contemporary Christianity quickly came to the surface," she said, "and each sees the other as a threat.

Conservative activists "are against abortion, sex education in the public schools, the teaching of evolution, the Equal Rights Amendment and nuclear disarmament," while liberal activists "were involved in housing, health care, human rights programs, education for social change, economic development and the peace movement."

These two religious worldviews are consistently at odds; the gap is so large that those in each camp often reject the idea that the other's concerns are "religious" at all: the Religious Right sees liberal support for social programs as a threat to freedom and a distraction from genuine moral concerns; liberals view the Religious Right's preoccupation with school prayer and pornography as a turning away from the religious concern for justice.

In another study, political scientists James Guth and John Green of Furman University in Greenville, South Carolina, found that religious contributors to political action committees (PACs) in 1980 were more active than less religious contributors—and that the pattern was consistent through Democratic, Republican, "right" and "left" PACs. Guth and Green asked PAC contributors to trace the history of their own political involvement back to 1960; they found that religious contributors were more active throughout the whole period. In 1980, they said, "If our respondents are any indication, the activity among Democrats and on the Left was more intensive among the religious than among the secular."

Guth and Green produced one really startling finding. While it came as no surprise that 32 percent of those newly active on the right cited the clergy as a "very important" source of political information, it was a surprise to find that 20 percent of those newly active in Democratic and left groups also cited the clergy. One reason Guth and Green were able to find religious activism across the political spectrum is that they focused on party and issue PACS; unlike conservative Christians, who organize as the "Moral Majority" or "Christian" groups, liberal religious activists more often organize as Democrats, women, environmentalists, or as members of unions or peace groups.

The most interesting recent study of the relationship between religion and politics is described in the book *Religion on Capitol Hill: Myths and Realities* by Peter L. Benson and Dorothy L. Williams. The two researchers from The Search Institute in Minneapolis, working with a grant from the National Endowment for the Humanities, did in-depth interviews with eighty members of Congress in the spring of 1980. At one level, the study produced some surprises. For example, it found that the members of Congress who are by most measures the least religious are not the most liberal members; in fact, they tend to be a little to the right of center. They also found that while 60 percent of the Evangelicals in Congress were conservative, a surprising 40 percent are liberal—"There are very few Evangelicals who take a moderate political position."

But the heart of *Religion on Capitol Hill* is its breakdown of six different kinds of religious belief—independent of denomination—found among the members of Congress and, presumably, among the general public. Based on an analysis of themes which came up in the extensive interviewing, Benson and Williams divided members of Congress up into these groups:

- *Legalistic religionists* (15 percent) "place very high values on rules, boundaries, limits, guidelines, direction and purpose."
- *Integrated religionists* (14 percent) show a balance on all value scales and have tested their faith—their "religious beliefs work to liberate, to free them to speak and act. . . . God, not humankind, is their audience."
- *Self-concerned religionists* (29 percent) are similar in belief to the legalists but are "almost entirely concerned with the relationship between the believer and God."
- *People-concerned religionists* (10 percent) "believe intensely that religious belief ought to move out to action . . . and that an important focus of that action should be on responding to the needs of the oppressed and the have-nots of the world."
- *Non-traditional religionists* (9 percent) are "very close to the people-concerned religionists, but have a much more symbolic, abstract sense of God."
- *Nominal religionists* (22 percent) have maintained formal church ties, but have little enthusiasm for religion; Benson and Williams suspect they may maintain religious affiliation for social and political expedience.

When Benson and Williams examined the voting records of members they interviewed according to liberal and conservative groups, they found that people-concerned and non-traditional religionists were always the first and second most liberal; legalistic and self-concerned religionists were always the first and second most conservative; integrated religionists were always the third most liberal; and nominal religionists were always the fourth most liberal. These studies suggest several conclusions:

1. While religious and political views seem to be linked, the relationship is complex. Anything short of the level of analysis used in the Benson-Williams study will be unreliable in predicting substantive positions.

2. There seems to be strong evidence that people who are more active religiously have more confidence in politics and other institutions and are more active politically than those who are less active religiously.

3. Religious political activists are by no means all, or even predominantly, conservative—a surprisingly large number of political liberals are also motivated by religious concerns.

PUBLIC OPINION

With the emergence of the Religious Right in 1980, pollsters have regularly surveyed national attitudes toward a number of issues involving religion and politics. There has been considerable consistency in their findings, as poll after poll showed a rejection of the partisan use of religion:

- In the fall of 1980, a Gallup Poll asked: "Certain religious groups are actively working for the defeat of political candidates who don't agree with their position on certain issues. Do you think they are right or wrong to do this?"; 28 percent said the religious groups were right, 60 percent said they were wrong.

- In an October 1980 NBC-Associated Press (AP) poll, only 3 percent of Americans said they had been "contacted by a church or religious group on behalf of any of the presidential candidates." Asked how they would react if they were so asked, 88 percent said it would make no difference, 3 percent said they would be more likely to vote for the candidate, and 8 percent said they would be less likely to vote for the candidate.

- A November 1980 *Los Angeles Times* poll asked, "Do you think organized religious groups should or should not endorse political candidates?"; 65 percent opposed endorsements, 35 percent supported them.

- An August 1981 NBC-AP poll asked, "Do you think churches and members of the clergy should be involved in politics, like backing a candidate for public office, or don't you think so?"; respondents opposed such involvement by 69 percent to 31 percent.

- A September 1984 Gallup Poll found that Americans opposed religious groups actively working to defeat political candidates by 52 percent to 30 percent and opposed religious efforts to change the law by 52 percent to 31 percent. Gallup found Americans said by 64 percent to 30 percent that it was wrong for members of the clergy to bring in their own political beliefs in sermons and by 54 percent to 39 percent for political candidates to bring in their own religious beliefs in discussing issues facing the nation.

  In a separate Gallup question, 3 percent of Americans said they had been asked by a member of the clergy to back a particular candidate and 1 percent said they had been asked to back a party. The responses from whites were 2 percent for a candidate and 1 percent for a party; for nonwhites it was 5 percent in each category. This racial breakdown indicates that although black churches have a long history of political involvement, white churches are still not heavily involved in partisan politics.

- An October 1984 Harris Poll found that Americans opposed preachers or bishops urging their members to vote against a political candidate opposed to a constitutional amendment on abortion by 69 percent to 27 percent and opposed their supporting a constitutional amendment on school prayer by 60 percent to 34 percent. Harris also found that Americans opposed Jerry Falwell's efforts to reelect Reagan by 59 percent to 24 percent. Feeling ran so high that only a bare 50 percent to 47 percent plurality of Americans supported the rights of the clergy to speak out in general on issues like abortion and school prayer.

- A poll conducted in late May and early June 1985 by Lance Tar-rance for Paul Weyrich's Free Congress Foundation found that among those who had voted for President Reagan in 1984, 44 per-cent had an unfavorable impression of Jerry Falwell and only 29 percent had a favorable opinion.
- An AP-Media General Poll released in October 1985 asked, "Do you think the separation of church and state is a good idea or not?"; 66 percent of respondents said it was a good idea, while 25 percent said it was not.
- A *Richmond Times-Dispatch* poll taken in fall 1985 showed that in his home state of Virginia, Falwell had a favorable rating of only 19 percent and a 62 percent unfavorable rating.

An important *Los Angeles Times* Poll conducted in the summer of 1986 went into considerable detail on the relationship of religion and politics. Reporter George Skelton summarized the poll's findings by saying, "Although most Americans today say they are religious and worried about declining standards of morality, they are in no mood to launch a moral crusade through the national political process."

An important part of the poll was its focus on the views of white Fundamentalists. The poll said 17 percent of Americans are Chris-tian Fundamentalists and that five in six of those are white. The poll defined Fundamentalists as those who believe "the Bible is the actual word of God and to be taken literally, word for word"; who have "tried to encourage someone to believe in Jesus Christ or to accept Him as their Savior" and "have been 'born again' or had a 'born again' experience."

Some key findings are particularly noteworthy.

- Both the total population (by 4 to 1) and the white Fundamental-ists (by 3 to 1) disapproved of "clergymen who preach political views in their sermons."
- The total sample objected to clergy who "work actively" for politi-cal candidates by a 4 to 3 margin, while white Fundamentalists were slightly opposed.

- The total sample disapproved of ministers running for political office by a 4 to 3 margin, while white Fundamentalists were evenly split. But opposition to ministers as candidates ran deeper than this.

The poll asked two groups of those interviewed to choose between two similar presidential candidates. In the first group, 40 percent "voted" for a fifty-five-year-old businessman who was born and raised in New York City and is married with two children; 35 percent "voted" for a sixty-year-old man who was born and raised in the Midwest and is married with one child. But, in the second group, the Midwesterner was also identified as a Protestant minister. In this group, he lost by 57 percent to 23 percent.

- Asked their views of candidates "who bring in their own religious beliefs when they discuss issues facing the nation," the total sample disapproved by 2.5 to 1, while white Fundamentalists were split on the question.

- Asked if they would be more or less likely to vote for "a political candidate who described himself as an evangelical Christian," the total sample said by 2.5 to 1 that they would be less likely to vote for such a candidate, while white Fundamentalists said by 3 to 1 that they would be more likely to vote for such a candidate. Some might be tempted to view the opposition among non-Fundamentalists to an Evangelical Christian candidate as a form of prejudice. But it may be that objections to Evangelical candidates reflect the view that those candidates would be more likely to "bring in their own religious beliefs when they discuss issues facing the nation."

These polls reveal some clear patterns:

1. Americans consistently oppose partisan political activity by religious leaders by a margin of about 2 to 1; such activity may well cause a backlash against candidates backed by those leaders. Even so, this means that a sizable minority of Americans—perhaps 30 percent—do support partisan, generally conservative, political activity by religious leaders. One lesson of American history is that an organized and highly motivated

minority can outweigh a lukewarm, unorganized majority. That is why, for example, gun control laws are so lax despite broad public support for tougher standards.

2. Despite the vast amount of attention given to ministers who are active in politics, only a handful of Americans report being urged to back a candidate by their minister. Most of this partisan activity is nothing new—it comes from black clergymen who have been involved in politics for years, especially on civil rights issues.

3. Americans do not want political candidates to make their private religious beliefs a campaign issue.

4. Evangelical Christians are by no means monolithic and by no means offer unqualified support for the Religious Right.

5. Americans clearly distinguish between questions of religious belief and questions of public morality.

RELIGIOUS VOTING PATTERNS

If religion didn't influence the way people vote, said election expert Richard Scammon, in a 1980 *Washington Star* article, then all religious groups would vote alike. But, he noted, they don't.

While knowing any one person's religious affiliation does not automatically reveal his or her political beliefs, religious affiliation has, historically, been tied to party affiliation and voting habits by culture and tradition; in the past Catholics have joked about their Democratic registration coming along with their baptismal certificate, and the Episcopal Church has been called the Republican Party at prayer, although neither of these characterizations is simply true today. Religion alone does not account for the differences in denominational voting patterns—differences in income, education, or region may play a role in those differences. But after these factors are taken into consideration, religion remains significant.

When commentators talk about political realignment, they are, whether they realize it or not, talking largely about shifts in religious voting patterns. In particular, gains among normally Democratic groups like Catholics and Evangelicals are largely responsible for Republican victories; at the same time, Democrats win when they hold these groups and make inroads among traditional Republican White Anglo-Saxon Protestant (WASP) voters. An examination of religious voting patterns bears this out.

CATHOLICS

Catholics make up the largest single denomination in the United States. According to the *Official Catholic Directory, (OCD)*, there are 52 million Catholics, about 22 percent of the population. Gallup Polls find that 27 percent of Americans—about 66 million people—identify themselves as Catholics. Using the lower *OCD* figures, these are key states with a large percentage of Catholics, with the number of electoral votes they had in 1984:

- Connecticut (8): 44.7 percent.
- Illinois (24): 31.5 percent.
- Louisiana (10): 31 percent.
- Massachusetts (13): 53 percent.
- New Jersey (16): 40.2 percent.
- New York (36): 35.6 percent.
- Pennsylvania (25): 32.7 percent.
- Wisconsin (11): 32 percent.

Catholics have been a key—though often unappreciated—element of the Democratic Party since the mid-nineteenth century. The Democrats wooed the massive influx of immigrants who came into the cities, providing human services at the precinct level at the same time the Republican Party was the home of the Know-Nothing movement of nativist anti-Catholics. The Catholic ties to the party were reinforced by the growth of the labor movement, which organized new immigrants and found its political home with the Democrats. One reason that Catholics were at home with the Democrats is that since the time of Pope Leo XIII in the late nineteenth century, the church had visibly been concerned with the plight of workers and comfortable with the involvement of government in economic affairs. Franklin Roosevelt's New Deal legislation closely paralleled the US Catholic bishops' 1919 program of reconstruction, which called for programs such as social security and unemployment insurance.

In 1928, the Democrats became the first party to nominate a Catholic—New York's Governor Al Smith—for the presidency. Smith lost after suffering anti-Catholic bias throughout the campaign. But he drew between 85 percent and 90 percent of the vote of Catholics and others in urban areas, setting the stage for Roosevelt's New Deal coalition. In 1932, Catholics voted for Roosevelt in about the same percentage they had voted for Smith, dropping off to about 73 percent in FDR's last two elections. Sixty-six percent voted for Harry Truman in the 1948 three-man race.

The Democratic stranglehold on Catholic votes was weakened by Dwight D. Eisenhower's landslide victories in 1952 and 1956. The popular World War II general held Democrat Adlai Stevenson to 55 percent of the Catholic vote in 1952 and a virtual standoff in 1956. In 1960, the Democrats nominated another Catholic, the young Massachusetts senator John F. Kennedy. A speech to Protestant ministers in Houston declaring his support for the separation of church and state reassured enough Protestants to keep the South in the Democratic column and Kennedy's 78 percent of the Catholic vote solidified the North and Midwest. In 1964, after Kennedy's assassination, Lyndon Johnson pulled 73 percent of the Catholic vote in his sweep of Barry Goldwater.

Hubert Humphrey—whose running mate, Edmund Muskie, was a Catholic—outpolled Richard Nixon 59 percent to 33 percent among Catholics in 1968, with 8 percent voting for third-party candidate George Wallace; but Nixon won a tight race with only 43 percent of the total vote. The largest Catholic defection since Stevenson occurred in 1972, when Catholics voted for Nixon by 52 percent to 48 percent over George McGovern. McGovern picked a popular Catholic senator, Thomas Eagleton of Missouri, as his running mate, but dropped him from the ticket after revelations about his past mental health problems—a move that could well have alienated some Catholic support, even though McGovern's final running mate, former Peace Corps and Office of Economic Opportunity director Sargent Shriver, was also a Catholic. Despite whatever advantage McGovern handed Nixon, Nixon built his campaign around appeals to northern Catholics and southern Evangelicals.

In 1976, the Democratic presidential candidate was former Georgia governor Jimmy Carter, a Southern Baptist Sunday school teacher. There was considerable talk during the campaign about Carter's "Catholic problem." In fact, there were two distinct Catholic problems. One was concern about how well Catholics would take to a Southern Baptist in light of the kind of anti-Catholicism associated with the South in Al Smith's day and later. The second problem was Carter's clash with the US Catholic bishops over the abortion issue; though Carter opposed federal funding for abortion, he also opposed a constitutional amendment to overturn the Supreme Court's 1973 decisions legalizing most abortions.

Statements by the bishops that they were "disappointed" by Carter's stand and "encouraged" by President Gerald Ford's support for a states' rights amendment created the impression that the bishops were endorsing Ford; the bishops put out a statement reaffirming their neutrality and advising Catholics to study a wide range of issues and to vote their conscience. Carter wanted a running mate who would appeal to Catholics and other traditional Democrats, and chose Minnesota Senator Walter Mondale, who was widely identified with Humphrey. On election day, Catholics returned to the Democratic Party, voting for Carter 57 percent to 41 percent over Ford, with 2 percent voting for independent candidate Eugene McCarthy (a Catholic).

In 1980, Ronald Reagan drew 51 percent of the Catholic vote—about the same as Eisenhower in 1956 and Nixon in 1972— but that amounted to a strong margin over Carter, who received only 40 percent of the Catholic vote; 9 percent voted for Independent candidate John Anderson. Abortion was not a significant issue in the election, although the Democratic National Committee believes it lost votes because of Carter's opposition to tuition tax credits for parents of private school students. The key factors appeared to be general dissatisfaction with Carter over the economy and the Iranian hostage situation and an empathy with Reagan, whose father was a Catholic; one observer said the 1980 race became one between a WASP (Carter) and a Catholic (Reagan). Despite this defection, however, Catholics remained heavily Democratic at the local level. In 1982, 59 percent of Catholics voted for Democratic congressional candidates.

About 55 percent of Catholics voted for Democratic congressional candidates in 1984, when Catholics gave Reagan a record 56 percent of their vote.

In the 1986 midterm elections, a CBS poll found 55 percent of Catholics voting for Democratic candidates, while an ABC poll said the figure was 61 percent.

Catholics have continued to drift back toward the Democratic Party and the Independent column, and away from the Republicans. In late 1984, Gallup surveys found that 44 percent of Catholics identified themselves as Democrats and 32 percent as Republicans. For the year 1986, it was 40 percent Democratic and 26 percent Republican. Catholics also lost a considerable amount of confidence in Reagan in the wake of revelations about the sale of arms to Iran and the use of the money raised for arms for the Nicaraguan Contras. Gallup surveys show that in July 1986 American Catholics strongly supported Reagan, with 66 percent saying they approved of his handling of the presidency and only 26 percent saying they disapproved. In January 1987 however, Catholics were evenly divided, with 46 percent approving of Reagan's job performance and 45 percent disapproving. In a trial heat for the 1988 presidential election in the same survey, Catholics supported then-candidate Democrat Gary Hart by a 52 percent to 36 percent margin over Vice President George Bush.

There is no doubt that a major contribution to the political "realignment" which occurred during the Reagan era was the shift of more than 10 percent of the Catholic presidential vote from the Democratic to Republican parties, proving once again that Democrats cannot take the votes of Catholics for granted. But, at the same time, consistent Catholic support for Democratic congressional candidates, gains in Democratic affiliation, and loss of confidence in Reagan suggest that the Catholic defection may have been no more permanent than past defections to Eisenhower and Nixon. Neither party can take Catholic support for granted, and Democrats have every reason to believe they can attract as much as 60 percent of the Catholic vote in 1988.

JEWS

"Jews," says Rabbi Arthur Hertzberg, past president of the American Jewish Congress, "may be the only group of 'haves' in America to vote to the left of their pocketbooks." There is no simple explanation for the continued preference of American Jews for liberal, usually Democratic, candidates. Like Catholic immigrants, Jews were wooed by urban Democratic ward heelers and formed the backbone of the labor movement. But American Jews also remain acutely aware of persecution against Jews in other countries and seem to find more sympathy for their minority status within more liberal circles. There have been some shifts among Jewish voters since 1972, but if the whole country has moved somewhat to the right since then, Jews remain to the left of center. Albert Vorspan, who heads the social action office of the Union of American Hebrew Congregations, the Reform branch of American Judaism, argues that, "By every poll and study, Jews are today—on abortion rights, ERA, affirmative action, nuclear freeze, civil liberties, defense budgets, etc.—the most liberal group in America."

While Jews make up less than 3 percent of the population, they are influential for two main reasons. First, they are heavy financial contributors—a 1985 study by the American Jewish Congress found that in 1984 Jews contributed half of the money raised by Democrats and one-fourth of the money raised by Republicans, who raise more money than the Democrats overall. Second, Jews are concentrated in key states and are more likely to vote than the general population. In 1980, almost 5 percent of all voters were Jewish; in New York State, where Jews make up 10.6 percent of the population, better than one voter in six was Jewish.

New York, with 36 electoral votes, has the largest percentage of Jews. Other key states are:

- New Jersey (16 electoral votes): 5.9 percent.
- Florida (21 electoral votes): 4.7 percent.
- Maryland (10 electoral votes): 4.6 percent.

- Massachusetts (13 electoral votes): 4.3 percent.
- Pennsylvania (25 electoral votes): 3.5 percent.
- California (47 electoral votes): 3.2 percent.

Jews voted heavily for Al Smith in 1928, giving him 70 percent to 75 percent of their vote. The Jewish vote for Franklin Roosevelt was 80 percent in 1932, 85 percent in 1936, 95 percent in 1940, and 92 percent in 1944. In 1948, Harry Truman received 65 percent to 70 percent of the Jewish vote, with another 15 percent voting for liberal third-party candidate Henry Wallace. Jews resisted the Eisenhower landslides, giving Adlai Stevenson 77 percent of their vote in 1952 and 75 percent in 1956. In 1960, 82 percent voted for John Kennedy, and 90 percent voted for Lyndon Johnson in 1964 against Barry Goldwater. Hubert Humphrey received 83 percent to 86 percent of the Jewish vote in 1968.

Jewish support fell significantly for George McGovern in 1972. It was partly a reflection of the general rejection of McGovern, and partly a reflection of concern that McGovern was soft on Israel; some Jews who shared McGovern's dovishness on Vietnam feared he wouldn't provide adequately for Israel's security. Nevertheless, McGovern received 66 percent of the Jewish vote. Jimmy Carter improved on that figure in 1976, getting 68 percent to 75 percent of the Jewish vote, despite some uneasiness about his "born-again" background.

But Jews turned on Carter in 1980: he received only 45 percent of their vote, with 40 percent going to Ronald Reagan and 15 percent to John Anderson. A survey conducted for the American Jewish Committee in 1984 asked Jews, regardless of who they voted for, who they wanted to be elected in 1980—the result was an astounding 53 percent to 47 percent preference for Reagan. Again, this reflected a general rejection of Carter in the wake of the Iranian hostage crisis, but it also reflected a widespread belief that Carter, after engineering the Camp David accords, had tipped toward the Arab states in his Middle East policy—a 1979 United Nations (UN) vote critical of Israel and UN Ambassador Andrew Young's private meetings with Palestine Liberation Organization (PLO) officials angered American Jews.

But Jews returned to old patterns in the 1982 midterm elections; according to network polls, they voted 72 percent to 20 percent for Democratic candidates, and 62 percent characterized their votes as "anti-Reagan."

In 1984, Jews—bucking a national trend—returned to the Democratic Party, giving Walter Mondale at least 66 percent of their votes. This was partly due to support for Mondale personally and partly due to Reagan's support from the Religious Right. In the 1986 midterm elections, CBS reported that 70 percent of Jews voted Democratic, while ABC reported that 79 percent did so.

There has been some erosion in Jewish identification with the Democrats in recent years; in 1976, according to Gallup, 56 percent said they were Democrats and 8 percent said they were Republicans, while in 1986, 50 percent said they were Democrats and 16 percent said they were Republicans. To the degree that there has been any political realignment among American Jews, it amounts to this: Jews remain overwhelmingly Democratic at the local level, and a Democratic presidential candidate probably shouldn't expect more than 70 percent of the Jewish vote.

PROTESTANTS

Political analysts have frequently focused on Catholic and Jewish voting patterns, but have paid far less attention to trends among and within American Protestants. As a result, important shifts have been missed and misinterpretations have been made. Part of the problem is that few observers paid much attention to Evangelicals until 1976, and data on voting patterns by denomination is difficult to come by. At the same time, pollsters don't always agree on how to define an "Evangelical," so it is often difficult to compare poll results. All Evangelicals are not Fundamentalists; generally, the more broadly the group is defined, the more Democratic it is; and the more narrowly it is defined, the more Republican it is.

One example of what the kind of confusion can lead to is the error made by A. James Reichley, the Brookings Institution's expert on religion and politics, in describing the shift among Evangelical voters from the Democratic to Republican Parties between 1976 and 1984. Reichley greatly overestimated the shift because he compared a figure of 58 percent of Southern Baptists who voted Democratic in 1976 with the 20 percent of all Evangelicals who voted Democratic in 1984. But Southern Baptists and Evangelicals are not identical; Southern Baptists make up only a percentage of Evangelicals, and about 40 percent of Southern Baptists do not describe themselves as "born-again Christians." In addition, Southern Baptists have traditionally been more Democratic than have Evangelicals. Evangelical Southern Baptists tend to be more blue collar, while Evangelicals in other denominations tend to be more middle class and more Republican oriented from the start.

This helps explain why, in 1976, 58 percent of Southern Baptists voted for Jimmy Carter while, according to precinct analyses conducted by Albert J. Menendez, author of *Religion at the Polls (1977)*, Carter's vote among all Evangelicals in 1976 was in the low- to mid-40 percent range. A decline from this level of the Evangelical vote to 20 percent is sufficient reason for concern for the Democrats, but it is still not as drastic as a decline from 58 percent to 20 percent. The fact that even the Democratic National Committee used the Reichley figures in a fund-raising letter indicates the party's continued lack of understanding of Evangelicals—and Southern Baptists.

Shifts in party preference by Evangelicals are important because during the New Deal era, through the election of the Baptist Harry Truman in 1948, white southern Evangelicals voted very much like black southern Evangelicals— Democratic. But, beginning with the election of President Dwight D. Eisenhower in 1952, southern Protestants have voted for Republican presidential candidates with great regularity, often while retaining Democratic registration and voting for local Democratic candidates.

Menendez notes that in 1956, Adlai Stevenson received 49.9 percent of the Baptist vote, running 7 percent ahead of his national showing among that group; in 1960, Menendez said, John Kennedy received 47.6 percent of the Baptist vote, about 2 percent below his national showing in a tight race. In 1964, Lyndon Johnson, while winning a landslide victory over Barry Goldwater, ran 13 percent behind his national showing among Baptists, with 48.7 percent of the Baptist vote.

It was Johnson's showing, more than that of the Catholic Kennedy, which foreshadowed a serious Baptist defection from the Democratic party at the presidential level; in 1968, the Democratic candidate, Hubert Humphrey, ran third among Baptists, almost 20 points below his national showing, with 24.2 percent, following 38.3 percent for Alabama governor George Wallace, running as an independent, and 37.5 percent for Richard Nixon. Humphrey, who almost won the three-man race, won only one southern state, Texas, where native Johnson's influence no doubt made the difference.

The conventional wisdom has been that the southern revolt against the Democratic leadership was sparked by the civil rights legislation of the Johnson era and a feeling that the South was being singled out for treatment. It would be difficult to find a reason other than race to explain the southern—and Southern Baptist—support for Goldwater and Wallace. A secondary factor may be that the South is the most hawkish section of the country. In 1972, Nixon's reelection largely reflected a rejection of George McGovern, but it also reflected a carefully designed strategy to woo both conservative Catholics and southerners, again, particularly Southern Baptists, who had voted for Wallace in 1968. Nixon wrapped himself in pious and patriotic rhetoric, appropriating two of the strongest symbols of the South, Billy Graham and the Grand Old Opry. While Southern Baptists are fairly liberal on economic issues, they also respond strongly to the "social issues," as Nixon painted McGovern as the candidate of "acid, abortion and amnesty." While Nixon was successful in holding McGovern to a standoff among Catholics, McGovern still ran some 10 points better among Catholics than among the nation at large; but he ran 13 percent weaker among Baptists than nationally, with a meager 25 percent of the Baptist vote.

Southern Baptists constituted the key swing vote in the 1976 presidential election when former Georgia governor Jimmy Carter, one of their own and a self-proclaimed "born-again Christian," won the Democratic nomination. In 1980, when the nation as a whole rejected Carter, he received about 40 percent of the Southern Baptist vote and 35 percent of the white Evangelical vote—enough that he lost by only a hair in most southern states, while winning in his home state of Georgia. While much was made of the efforts of the Religious

Right to influence Evangelical Christians in 1980, Carter actually ran 2 percent better among Evangelical Protestants than among mainline Protestants.

In the 1982 midterm elections, Evangelicals joined mainline Protestants again in voting heavily Republican. In the 1984 elections, Evangelicals voted more heavily Republican than did mainline Protestants: 81 percent of white born-again Protestants voted for President Reagan.

In the 1986 midterm elections, a CBS-*New York Times* Poll found that 69 percent of self-designated white Evangelicals or Fundamentalists voted for Republican candidates nationwide. A survey of voters in four southern states where Republicans incumbents were defeated by Democrats—Alabama, Florida, Georgia, and North Carolina—found that between 60 percent and 69 percent of white Evangelicals voted Republican. Some polls showed lower turnout among Evangelicals than in 1984, as they made up only 12 percent of those voting, down from 17 percent in the previous election. At the same time, Democrats received between 43 percent and 47 percent of the votes of all white Protestants; given the still-high Republican support among white Evangelicals, this means that a majority of mainline white Protestants voted for Democratic candidates.

In the January 1987 Gallup Poll, Gary Hart registered a stunning turnaround against George Bush among Evangelicals in a trial heat for 1988. In July 1986, Bush had led Hart by 53 percent to 39 percent among all Evangelicals (including blacks and Hispanics); but in January, Hart led Bush in this group by 48 percent to 41 percent.

To sum up, the large-scale shift of Evangelical voters from the Democratic to Republican Party has been the major source of political realignment in recent decades. But even this "shift" is not simple. Several facts must be kept in mind:

- It is simplistic to identify white Evangelicals with Southern Baptists, who continue to be more Democratic.

- The degree of the Republican shift is easy to overestimate; northern white Evangelicals have been predominantly Republican for decades and southern white Evangelicals have voted Republican at the presidential level for almost as long.

• Democrats do not need to win a majority of white Evangelical votes to carry the South; they need only a respectable minority. They have had difficulty managing even that, but the closeness of the 1980 presidential race in the South and the 1986 Senate elections make it clear that a Democrat who can win more than about 35 percent of the white Evangelical vote has an excellent chance of carrying the South.

It's useful to look at Protestant voting patterns in terms of specific denominations.

Baptists

Baptists, who make up 20 percent of the population, are among the most Democratic groups in terms of political affiliation, although there has been some Republican drift in recent years. In 1976, 57 percent of all Baptists were Democrats and 17 percent Republicans; in 1986, it was 50 percent Democratic, 27 percent Republican. About 30 percent of all Baptists are blacks, the most Democratic group in the country.

Methodists

Methodists, 9 percent of the population, have shifted strongly toward the Republicans in recent years. In 1976, 45 percent were Democrats, 30 percent Republican; in 1986, it was 38 percent Republican, 34 percent Democratic. In 1976, Methodists split 50-50 between Carter and Ford. In 1980, according to the University of Michigan National Election Survey, 53 percent voted for Reagan, 40 percent for Carter, and 5 percent for John Anderson. In 1984, 65 percent voted for Reagan and 35 percent for Mondale.

Lutherans

Lutherans, 5 percent of the population, have experienced a shift similar to that of Methodists. In 1976, 35 percent were Republicans and 35 percent Democrats; in 1986, it was 43 percent Republican, 29 percent Democratic. Fifty-two percent of Lutherans voted for Carter in 1976, and Lutherans were relatively cool to Reagan in 1980; 56 percent voted for Reagan, 31 percent for Carter and 12 percent for

Anderson. In 1984, however, 66 percent voted for Reagan, 34 percent for Mondale.

Presbyterians

Presbyterians, 2 percent of the population, are heavily Republican in registration. In 1976, 39 percent were Republican and 32 percent Democratic; in 1986, it was 53 percent Republican, 22 percent Democratic. In 1980, 67 percent voted for Reagan, 24 percent for Carter, and 7 percent for Anderson. In 1984, 68 percent voted for Reagan, 32 percent for Mondale.

Episcopalians

Like Presbyterians, Episcopalians are staunchly Republican in registration. In 1976, 38 percent were Republican and 27 percent Democratic; in 1986, it was 44 percent Republican, 26 percent Democratic. In 1980, 69 percent of Episcopalians voted for Reagan, 25 percent voted for Carter, and 6 percent voted for John Anderson. In 1984, however, Reagan actually lost some ground among Episcopalians, getting 60 percent of their vote while Mondale received 40 percent, a 15-percentage-point gain over Carter's 1980 showing.

United Church of Christ

The United Church of Christ, which represents 2 percent of the population, is also heavily Republican. In 1986, 45 percent were registered as Republicans, 30 percent as Democrats.

Disciples of Christ (Christian Church)

The Disciples of Christ, concentrated in the West and Midwest, also make up 2 percent of the population. In 1986, 39 percent were registered as Democrats, 37 percent as Republicans.

MORMONS AND THE UNCHURCHED

Two other religious groups deserve mention. One is the Mormons, a rapidly growing denomination representing 2 percent of the population generally, but 13 percent in the Rocky Mountain States. Mormons were once blue-collar Democrats, but have become very heavily Republican in recent years. Democrats may be making a comeback of sorts within this group, however; in 1986, according to Gallup, 33 percent said they were Republicans and 28 percent said they were Democrats.

The "unchurched"—those who claim no religious affiliation— are a "religious group" with growing influence. According to Gallup Polls, this group now makes up 8 percent of the population. It tends to be made up of well-educated young people, mostly men, who tend to be concentrated in New England and on the West Coast. In 1986, 31 percent were Democrats, 26 percent Republicans. In 1976, the unchurched voted 59 percent to 41 percent for Jimmy Carter. In 1980, according to an ABC poll, they voted 40 percent for Carter, 38 percent for Reagan, 17 percent for Anderson, and 5 percent for "other." In 1984, they favored Mondale by 53 percent to 47 percent.

CONCLUSIONS

When there is a Republican or Democratic trend in the country, different religious groups are more or less resistent; political realignment involves shifts in party preferences among those religious groups. Republican successes in recent years have been due primarily to attracting normally Democratic Catholic and white Evangelical voters; but it has also involved attracting support from the "middle-ground" Protestants, Methodists, and Lutherans.

But the fact that a trend has occurred does not mean that it has become institutionalized. There are clear signs that Catholics are getting ready to "come home" to the Democratic Party in 1988. The Republicans seem to have a firmer hold on white Evangelicals; but the 1986 midterm elections suggest that the difference between getting 80 percent of that vote and 70 percent—and voter turnout—is the difference between winning and losing. At the same time, the Republicans' consistent wooing of Catholics and Evangelicals may be undermining their base with mainline Protestants. Despite a heavy increase in Republican affiliation, mainline Protestants were willing to vote for Democratic candidates for governor, House, and Senate in

1986—and a Democratic defection here could be disastrous for the Republicans.

It's no wonder, then, that political candidates from both parties have developed a keen interest in religious voting patterns. Successful politicians in America appeal to candidates on three levels: as Americans, as individuals, and as members of intermediate groups or "tribes." Americans have agendas as blacks, farmers, homeowners, women, doctors, or members of other groups, including religious groups. Candidates legitimately look for ways to appeal to Jews, urban Catholics, or rural Evangelicals; the challenge they face is to do so on the basis of common interests which are not at odds with the common good, without making divisive appeals to sectarian views.

3. The 1984 Election

"Are You Running With Me, Jesus?"

The 1984 election provides a particularly worthwhile case study of the relationship between religion and politics in America. The presence of religion in the election was unique in its degree and variety; it was a factor in both parties and a major issue in the presidential election itself. It also involved players and issues that will play a major role in the 1988 election—and beyond.

GOD AS CAMPAIGN CHAIRMAN

Before the first primary of 1984, it became clear that religion would be a campaign issue during the coming presidential campaign. The reason was simple: Lou Cannon, a *Washington Post* reporter who had covered Ronald Reagan since his days as governor of California, wrote on February 13 that "in the first weeks of his reelection campaign, the incumbent seems to have made the Lord his honorary chairman."

Cannon noted that Reagan had mentioned God ten times in his recent State of the Union Address, twenty-four times in a speech to the National Religious Broadcasters, and had consistently identified God with the Republican Party. Cannon wrote,

In addition to being silly, the suggestion that God somehow is a 'value' of Republicans more than of their opponents makes mincemeat of any distinction between church and state. It raises doubts about Reagan's commitment to religious values he espouses. It cheapens values it extols by taking the private and serious matter of religion and the important question of school prayer and plunging them into a partisan context.

Reagan was taught as a child that God is the ruler of nations, greater than any king or president. Does he think he is honoring God by reducing him to the status of a Reagan advance man?

There was no small irony in Reagan's emergence as champion of God and family values: He had been divorced; he rarely saw his grandchildren; he attended church barely a dozen times in his first term as president; as governor, he signed the most liberal abortion bill in the country before turning into a "pro-lifer." He identified himself with Catholic concerns before Catholic audiences and with Evangelical concerns before Evangelical audiences.

Reagan's biography made him uniquely suited to implement a campaign approach followed by Republican presidential candidates since Richard Nixon—combining appeals to normally Democratic Catholics and Evangelicals. Reagan's compatibility with Catholics was part of his birthright; his father was an Irish Catholic, and Reagan retained an essentially Irish demeanor that made him a comfortable figure to American Catholics.

Reagan's appeal to Evangelicals developed in a different way. In the mid-1960s, he became close to a number of fundamentalists in California, including singer Pat Boone. Journalist Ronnie Dugger, in the *Philadelphia Inquirer,* October 21, 1984, reported that in 1970, Reagan, Boone, and a number of other Evangelicals held a prayer meeting in Reagan's home. Evangelist George Otis said that the session turned into a prophesy in which God spoke through him and told Reagan, "I have watched you and I have been pleased . . . and if you walk in my ways, it is my will that you become president at 1600 Pennsylvania Avenue." Otis told Dugger that Herbert Ellingwood, a Reagan aide who was present, later told him that Reagan looks back at that session as a benchmark.

The strategy of targeting Catholics and Evangelicals involved taking specific positions on three social issues: support for a constitutional amendment to overturn the Supreme Court decisions legalizing most abortions; support for another amendment overturning the court's ban on government-sponsored vocal school prayer; and support for tuition tax credits for parents of students in private schools.

Once he was in the White House, Reagan put forward initiatives in all three areas, but none was ever enacted. Midway through his first term, Reagan was criticized by a number of Religious Right leaders for not pushing hard enough for their agenda and giving the social issues lower priority than his economic program of tax and budget cuts and increased military spending. Reagan was willing to advance the social agenda, but not at the expense of higher priorities and not at the expense of a loss in popularity or prestige.

The most vivid example of this was a controversy involving the question of tax-exempt status for religious schools which discriminate on the basis of race. The Supreme Court was preparing to hear two related cases, one involving the Fundamentalist Bob Jones University in South Carolina and one involving the Goldsboro Christian Schools in North Carolina. Basically, the schools admitted that their policies discriminated on the basis of race, but argued that that discrimination was based on deeply held religious beliefs; therefore, they said, they should not be denied tax-exemption. Religious Right leaders made the Bob Jones case a top priority; the movement had received significant impetus in 1978 when it mobilized against Internal Revenue Service (IRS) efforts to strengthen regulations on antidiscriminatory policies in tax-exempt private schools.

At first, the Reagan administration indicated that it would support the schools in their challenge to the IRS. But, after immediate criticism from civil rights groups and moderates in both parties, the administration reversed itself and supported the IRS, provoking considerable anger within the Religious Right. The court eventually ruled 8 to 1 that the IRS had the right to deny tax-exemption to the schools; all nine justices agreed that the IRS requirement of antidiscriminatory policy as a cost of tax-exemption did not violate the schools' First Amendment rights.

If Reagan disappointed the Religious Right on the Bob Jones case, however, he certainly escalated his rhetoric on their behalf. He continued to refer to Christians as "we" and members of all other faiths as "they." He proclaimed 1983 "The Year of the Bible." He tolerated a White House aide, religious liaison Carolyn Sundseth, who said that all those in the White House should "get saved or get out." He told the National Religious Broadcasters, "Within the covers of that simple book [the Bible] are all the answers to all the problems that face us today—if we'd only read and believe." He told the National Association of Evangelicals that passage of his school prayer amendment "would do more than any other action to reassert the faith and values that made America great."

Reagan's religious rhetoric served a political purpose, but it also reflected his belief in his own chosenness. Reagan's pastor in Bel Air, California, the Rev. Donn Moomaw, told Dugger, "I really do think he has a sense of being divinely appointed to the task, not just elected to the task, and that God has something to do with it. He really feels that he's been ordained to this task."

That attitude was reflected in Reagan's rhetoric as he spoke of his election in 1980 as a spiritual turning point for America. "In recent years," he told the National Association of Evangelicals in early 1984,

we must admit, America did seem to lose her religious and moral bearings, to forget that faith and values are what made us good and great. . . . The American people decided to put a stop to that long decline. And today our nation is seeking a rebirth of freedom and faith, a great national renewal. . . . But this renewal is more than material. America has begun a spiritual awakening. Faith and hope are being restored. Americans are turning back to God. Church attendance is up. . . . Today, Americans from Maine to California are seeking His face. And I do believe that He has begun to heal our blessed land.

Reagan's rhetoric prompted an unusual exchange of letters between Reagan and Norman Lear, representing People for the American Way. Lear wrote Reagan to say, "I am deeply troubled by what seems to be an endorsement of the 'Christian Nation Movement' in many of your recent speeches"; and, "I am concerned that you not use the office of the presidency as 'Evangelist-in-Chief,' or to further the notion that any particular group of Americans is to be accorded special standing because they practice any religion."

Reagan replied on May 22 that, "until I read your letter, I was unaware of any 'Christian Nation Movement,' and I certainly do not support the notion that any group of citizens is to be accorded special standing 'because they practice any religion.' "

He continued that, "I do believe the first amendment is being somewhat distorted or misinterpreted by some who would, by government decree, make freedom *of* religion into freedom *from* religion" and relayed an anecdote about a child who was forbidden to say a blessing before lunch in the school cafeteria. He said, "I believe that Madalyn Murray O'Hair, who brought about the anti-school prayer decision, was imposing her atheism on those of us who believe in God."

Lear replied to Reagan's letter, noting that, "The issue is not, as you suggest, between atheists and believers. It is the imposition of a creed on citizens through the powers and public role of the government—whether that creed be Christianity, Judaism, Buddhism, or atheism. It is not the substance of what is imposed—but the imposition itself—that is objectionable to a free people."

Lear criticized Reagan's

assumption of a governmental role of Evangelist-in-Chief. By this, I mean your use of the ceremonial and official powers of the Presidency to validate one set of religious beliefs over another. In doing so, you say to those Americans who do not share your particular religious beliefs that they are second-class citizens. As you said in a recent newspaper interview, "We have respected every other religion. They're free to practice in our country."

Mr. President, there are not "other" religions in "our" country. America belongs to *all* its citizens, no matter what their religions. No faith has a special patrimony in the eyes of the Constitution.

Reagan replied, "I am not using this office as a pulpit for one religion above all others, but I do subscribe to George Washington's remark regarding high moral standards, decency, etc., and their importance to civilization and his conclusion that to have these without religion as a base was to ask for the impossible."

Reagan's denials notwithstanding, his behavior in office showed that religion played two roles in his political career. First, through a sense of being chosen by God for his role, Reagan identified himself with God; for Ronald Reagan, the moral thing to do was what he wanted to do. Second, religion was a campaign tool to be used for partisan ends.

THE DEMOCRATIC PRIMARIES

Despite Republican efforts to stake out a political monopoly on religion, a quick survey of the eight Democrats running in the 1984 presidential primaries revealed that no such monopoly exists. The collection of ministers, minister's sons, and former divinity students sometimes looked as much like a bunch of choirboys as a group of would-be presidential candidates.

Even the least overtly religious of the group, Senator Alan Cranston of California, argued the major issue of his campaign—the nuclear freeze—in moral terms. Cranston, sixty-nine, is one of the most liberal members of the Senate. He lists his religious affiliation as "Protestant," a generic identification that indicates lack of affiliation with any particular denomination. Cranston's press secretary, Murray Flander, says, "He's a very religious man in the sense that Abraham Lincoln was religious. He has a very profound sense of the sacredness of life and the existence of God."

The most religiously conservative candidate, former Florida governor Reuben Askew, fifty-five, seemed to be trying to position himself as 1984's Jimmy Carter—a moderate, Evangelical southerner. Askew was raised as a Christian Scientist, but became a Presbyterian when he married his wife, Donna Lou, in 1956. Both are elders in the church. Askew sought support from Evangelicals during his short-lived campaign. In Florida, he had supported evangelistic campaigns led by both Billy Graham and Bill Bright, head of the Campus Crusade for Christ, and had supported Anita Bryant's campaign to oppose gay rights in Florida. In 1972, he campaigned against a nonbinding school prayer amendment referendum which carried by a 3 to 1 margin in Florida. Askew supported legislation barring abortion except in the case of rape, incest, or danger to the mother's health; that earned him some support from right-to-life groups in the Iowa caucuses.

Another dark-horse candidate who failed to last beyond the early primaries was Senator Ernest Hollings of South Carolina. Hollings, a Lutheran, supported a school prayer amendment, but was best-known in religious circles for his ardent opposition to tuition tax credits for church-run schools. He was popular with the press during the campaign for his frankness and quick wit, but both often went beyond the bounds of acceptable political debate. Hollings had already angered many Jews when, in a Senate floor debate, he referred to Senator Howard Metzenbaum (D-Ohio) as "the senator from

B'nai B'rith." But Hollings's harshest public comments on religion have been directed at the Catholic church. During the 1978 tax credit debate, Senator Daniel Patrick Moynihan (D-New York), a tax credit sponsor, accused Hollings of ridiculing Catholic schools. Hollings drew criticism from South Carolina Catholic leaders in November 1983 when he attacked the US Catholic bishops' lobbying on behalf of tax credits. He charged on the Senate floor that the bishops were "running around the hallways" acting like "a bunch of kids" in pushing for tax credits; he called their lobbying a "disgrace."

George McGovern's religious roots were familiar to most Americans who remembered his 1972 landslide defeat by Richard Nixon. McGovern's father was a Wesleyan Methodist minister; McGovern attended Garrett Theological Seminary in Evanston, Illinois, and was a student preacher at a Methodist church in Diamond Lake, Illinois, before he turned to politics. McGovern's prairie populism was shaped by the Social Gospel movement of the early twentieth century, which preached the necessity of progressive social policy. McGovern's opposition to the Vietnam War was a moral crusade. One observer called his "Come Home, America" acceptance speech "pure Methodist Federation for Social Action." McGovern's greatest impact on the 1984 campaign came in one line when he urged Iowa's caucus voters, "Don't throw away your conscience."

John Glenn's religious roots were less visible than those of most other primary candidates and he seldom used overtly religious rhetoric, but his old-fashioned patriotism and astronaut heroism seemed to convey a sense of piety. Glenn was raised in a strict Presbyterian family; in 1962, he said, "My religion is not one of the fire engine type—not one to be called on in an emergency and then put God back in the woodwork." On the "religious issues," Glenn opposed constitutional amendments on abortion and school prayer and opposed tuition tax credits, but he also opposed gay rights.

The most unusual religious background of the Democratic candidates belonged to Senator Gary Hart of Colorado, who had undergone a pilgrimage from Fundamentalism to liberal Protestantism—like Cranston, he too listed his religious preference only as "Protestant," although he occasionally attended a Presbyterian church. A further step in Hart's pilgrimage was suggested in July 1984, when a *Vanity Fair* article by Gail Sheehy reported that a Native American woman named Marilyn Youngblood was Hart's "spiritual advisor"; Hart denied it.

Hart was best known as George McGovern's campaign manager in 1972 and as a leader of the antiwar movement. He was first elected to the Senate in 1974 as part of the post-Watergate reaction. He maintained a liberal voting record, but was not always predictable. He pulled the upset of the campaign by beating Mondale in the New Hampshire primary and almost forcing him out of the race before slim victories in Alabama and Georgia gave the former vice president a chance to deal with the Hart challenge.

Hart was raised in a strict Church of the Nazarene family in Kansas; his mother, a Sunday school teacher, wanted him to become a minister in the denomination, which, while an offshoot of Methodism, was essentially Fundamentalist. The church forbade smoking, drinking, movie going, and slow dancing. Hart attended Bethany Nazarene College in Oklahoma City. There Hart, who had been struggling with his religion, met Prescott Johnson, a professor who introduced him to the world of philosophy, including Plato and Kierkegaard. Johnson, himself a Nazarene, later spoke of Hart's "turmoil" at dealing with the church's "frozen dogma."

Inspired by Johnson, Hart entered Yale University Divinity School, a world apart from the Church of the Nazarene; he later switched to Yale's law school. Hart's break with his religion was only one of his many efforts to break with his past—he was symbolic of millions of Americans whose path to success was based on escaping from their roots. Columnist David Broder noted that generational conflict was a consistent theme in Hart's political career—his 1974 slogan in Colorado was, "They had their turn. Now it's our turn."

"The message that leaps from Hart's personal history," Broder wrote,

is that his generational conflict began with his family. His parents were poor, hard-working, lightly-educated Kansans named Hartpence, who were deeply influenced by their strict fundamentalist religious beliefs. Before he was in his mid-20s, Hart had changed his name, left his religious practice, studied at two graduate schools at Yale and set his sights on a new life among the upwardly mobile and high-living young professionals flocking to Denver.

But, in a sense, Hart never broke completely with his past. Colorado governor Richard Lamm said, "A lot of Gary can be explained by his theological upbringing. He feels a calling. He's a man with a mission." Hart's campaign certainly had the zeal of a religious crusade. He mocked the Fundamentalist right and called on a higher vision of morality—the Watergate era morality with which he was most comfortable. He had only one reference to religion in his standard stump speech: "I am surprised and amazed that a president who adopts the agenda of the Moral Majority has for three years condoned a systematic pattern of unethical behavior on the part of more than fifty top members of his administration."

The paradox of Hart running from his past while carrying it with him helped account for his support—he ran best among the now-famous "Yuppies" who shared his flight and among Evangelicals and other Protestants. Hart's emphasis on individualism and his attack on "special interest groups" reflected the radical individualism of his Fundamentalist background; at the same time, he showed no awareness that Yuppies were every bit as much of an interest group as labor and no shame at wooing Jews as an interest group in primaries in Florida, New York, and California. For a time, it seemed the only issue being addressed in the New York primary was whether the United States should move its Israeli embassy to Jerusalem. Jewish organizations were fully committed to the move, as was former vice president Walter Mondale; Hart had reservations about it, but later backed the move. Mondale sensed a political advantage in catching Hart in a "flip-flop" and pressed the issue on that level. Even some Jewish leaders complained privately that both candidates were "pandering" to Jews.

Mondale, like McGovern, is the son of a Methodist minister. Finley Lewis wrote in *Mondale* that the former vice president and his two brothers "were imbued with their father's Social Gospel notions about mutual responsibilities of church and state in seeking a maximum well-being—spiritual, economic and social—of those they served." Mondale says he went into politics to serve other people because of his faith.

As a senator and vice president, Mondale had an excellent working relationship with mainline religious leaders; he treated them as a legitimate interest group to be courted as part of a coalition needed to pass housing, education, and other social justice legislation. He faced a foretaste of the Religious Right in 1975 when he and Representative John Brademas (D-Indiana) were trying to pass a major bill to provide federal aid for day-care centers. Conservative church leaders attacked the bill as federal intrusion into the family and leveled a series of spurious charges against it. Mondale turned for help to state Catholic conferences, the Baptist Joint Committee for Public Affairs and other church groups; they delivered a series of statements that seemed to neutralize the attacks, although the bill eventually failed, primarily because of its cost.

Mondale took predictable Democratic positions on the "religious issues"—he opposed abortion and school prayer amendments and tuition tax credits and supported a gay rights bill. But he also went out of his way to find common ground on some of those issues. He backed a bill written by Cranston to facilitate adoption as an alternative to abortion. He also pushed legislation to guarantee that students in church-run and other private schools had access to all federal education programs for which they were eligible; he earned the enmity of Griffin Bell, Carter's first Attorney General, by moving the administration to support the use of CETA public service workers in church-run schools.

Mondale's emphasis on personal relationships carried over to his relationships with religious leaders. He was involved in one of the few unreported moments of Pope John Paul II's 1979 US visit. Mondale had become friends with his Washington, D.C. neighbor, Archbishop Jean Jadot, the Vatican's apostolic delegate to the church in the United States. In the evening after the pope visited Carter at the White House, he and Jadot paid a private half-hour visit to Mondale and his family at their home.

The most overtly religious—and most controversial—Democrat in the primaries was the Reverend Jesse Jackson, at forty-two the best-known and most popular black leader in the country. Jackson attended the Chicago Theological Seminary before joining the

Southern Christian Leadership Conference to work with Martin Luther King, Jr. Jackson too opposed school prayer and tuition tax credits; he had in the past opposed federal funding for abortion, but reversed his position during the primaries, a change the National Association of Evangelicals called "an unconscionable willingness to put politics before convictions."

Jackson had become increasingly visible—and enigmatic—in recent years. There often seemed to be two Jesse Jacksons. One was the founder of Operation PUSH, a program to help motivate black teenagers to get an education, the eloquent spokesman for the poor and minorities. One of Jackson's best lines of the campaign was a joint attack on Reagan's school prayer amendment and school lunch cuts. Reagan, he charged, didn't even understand the structure of prayer—"you pray for that which you are about to receive, not for that which has just been taken away."

The first Jesse Jackson came up with an inspiring campaign theme, the creation of a "Rainbow Coalition" of black, white, red, brown, and yellow Americans working together. But the second Jesse Jackson—a hip-shooting radical whose rhetoric included more than a trace of anti-Semitism—made the realization of the Rainbow Coalition impossible. Both Jesse Jacksons insured that the first black to run for president in a major party primary dominated media coverage of the campaign; the Mondale-Hart struggle that developed often took a back seat to Jackson's latest activity.

Jackson also dominated the religious dimension of the primaries. The first issue was his use of black churches for fundraising. "What labor was supposed to be for Mondale and I guess what big business is for Reagan, the black church has been to this campaign," Jackson told ABC's "Nightline" program. "Big Church" was the backbone of Jackson's campaign—ministers played key organizational roles and enthusiastically passed the hat. The Rev. T. J. Jemison, president of the National Baptist Convention USA, which pledged $100,000 to Jackson's campaign, told *The New York Times*, "The black church is the springboard of Rev. Jackson's campaign. Its support, morally, spiritually, and financially, is the thing keeping him near the top in the polls."

The *Times* reported that black churches in California raised $200,000 for Jackson in one day and reported this service:

At the Bethel Baptist Institutional Church in Jacksonville, Fla., Mr. Jackson reportedly raised $9,000 in checks and cash. The donations followed a sermon-like appeal by the candidate, who asked those in the congregation wanting to pledge $1,000 to come forward, followed by those wanting to donate $500, $100 and finally $50. The pleas were followed by passing collection plates for contributions under $50.

That kind of activity set off charges of a "double standard"—why, it was asked, was it all right for black preachers to endorse and raise money for Jackson, but not for white Fundamentalists to endorse and raise funds for Reagan? In fact, at least some black pastors seem to have violated Internal Revenue Service policy on political involvement. The IRS says that a pastor may endorse a candidate from the pulpit if he is speaking for himself; but if the endorsement comes on behalf of a church structure—a congregation or a denomination—it violates the tax code. But the black churches also seemed immune from prosecution—it would be impossible for the IRS to go after them without appearing to harass Jackson or without having to also go after Fundamentalist churches distributing "biblical" voting scorecards and otherwise endorsing candidates—including, of course, the incumbent president of the United States.

Jackson offered a symbol of hope to young blacks, bringing many who had never voted before into the system. But his appeals triggered widespread talk of a white backlash, particularly in the South. The major reason is that Jackson did not run as a candidate who happened to be black; he ran as a candidate asking support because he was black. He spoke of "reciprocal voting": because blacks have voted for white candidates, he argued, the time had come for whites to vote for a black—presumably, whether they wanted to or not. He constantly discovered new litmus tests for racism: Jackson argued that the runoff system—in which the top candidates face off if no candidate receives 50 percent of the vote in a state primary—violated the Voting Rights Act, a novel interpretation which failed to convince the majority of party leaders. The white backlash was real; Lamarr Mooneyham, president of the North Carolina Moral Majority, said in May,

"If I could afford to pay Jesse, I'd bring him down here every month."

Jackson began his campaign with particularly strained relations with American Jewish leaders, who cited a number of troubling incidents: praise for PLO leader Yasser Arafat; the comment, "I am sick and tired of hearing about the Holocaust"; a charge that the Jewish community pressured President Carter into removing Andrew Young as US ambassador to the United Nations after it was disclosed that Young had held private meetings with PLO officials; a call for an end to US economic and military aid to Israel after Israel invaded Lebanon in 1982.

On February 13, 1984, *The Washington Post* ran a lengthy article by Rick Atkinson outlining tensions between Jackson and Jews. Buried deep in the piece was a bombshell—"In private conversations with reporters, Jackson has referred to Jews as 'Hymie' and to New York as 'Hymietown.' "

Atkinson wrote that Jackson, when confronted with the charge, said, "I'm not familiar with that. That's not accurate." The *Post* revealed February 22 that the source for the "Hymie" quotes was one of its own reporters, Milton Coleman, a black political writer covering Jackson's campaign. Jackson continued to say he could not recall making the remark. On February 22, he complained of "being hounded, pursued, and persecuted" by some Jewish groups. The militant Jewish Defense League had launched a Jews Against Jackson campaign with an ad in *The New York Times,* but major Jewish organizations—particularly Hyman Bookbinder, Washington representative of the American Jewish Committee—had dissociated themselves from the group.

The issue escalated again on February 25 with the emergence of Jackson's most controversial supporter, Minister Louis Farrakhan, the little-known head of the Nation of Islam, a militant, separatist offshoot of the Black Muslim movement in the United States. Introducing Jackson at the Nation of Islam's annual "Savior's Day" celebration, Farrakhan said, "I say to the Jewish people who may not like our brother, when you attack him, you attack the millions of others who line up with him. You are attacking all of us. If you harm this brother, I warn you in the name of Allah, this will be the last one you do harm."

Farrakhan, who had accompanied Jackson on his trip to Syria, had a long history of racial animosity. He became a Black Muslim in the 1950s when the movement favored separatism. He served as assistant to Malcolm X when he ran mosques in Boston and, later, Harlem. Farrakhan remained with the Muslims after Malcolm left in a dispute with Elijah Mohammad, the movement's leader. But Farrakhan himself split from the movement in 1978 after its new leader, Elijah's son Warid D. (Wallace) Mohammad, introduced radical changes— he abandoned the black nationalist stance and urged his followers to become part of the American system; he even invited whites to join. Farrakhan left what was now called the American Muslim Mission, with about 100,000 members, to form the Nation of Islam, with about 10,000 members. He continued to promote black separatism and urged his followers to stay out of the political system until he endorsed Jackson; Farrakhan's security arm, the Fruit of Islam, provided security for Jackson until he qualified for Secret Service protection.

On February 27, Jackson finally admitted his "Hymie" remarks and apologized for them at a synagogue in Manchester, New Hampshire. He said that he had at first said he could not recall the comments because they had been made in an off-hand manner in a private conversation. But he said he was speaking out now because the remark had obscured the major issues in his campaign.

But even in apologizing, Jackson managed to make himself appear the injured party. He blamed Coleman for reporting his remarks and Jews for being offended. He said "An off-color remark has no bearing on religion or politics," a surprising remark in light of the fact that Interior Secretary James Watt had recently been forced from office because he had made just such a remark about members of a department advisory committee. "We must forgive and redeem," Jackson said. "Human to err, divine to forgive. I feel good tonight. Suffering brings redemption." Any politician will try to turn adversity to political advantage, but Jackson's effort to turn a less-than-convincing apology for a bigoted remark into a pat on his own back for his suffering set, in the view of some, a new standard for the self-serving use of religion in politics.

Jewish leaders were cautious in accepting Jackson's apology. Howard Friedman, president of the American Jewish Committee, called on him to reexamine other troubling statements he had made about Jews. Nathan Perlmutter of the Anti-Defamation League of B'nai B'rith said, "The bona fides of his remorse would be enhanced . . . by a public disavowal of Muslim leader Louis Farrakhan's demagogic appeal to class hatred."

Farrakhan upped the ante again in a March 11, 1984, radio broadcast. First, he threatened Milton Coleman: Although he said, "At this point, no physical harm," Farrakhan also said, "One day soon we will punish you with death. You're saying 'When is that?' In sufficient time. We will come to power inside this country one day soon. And the white man is not going to stop us from executing the law of God on all of you who fall under our jurisdiction." (Jackson later described his reaction to Farrakhan's statements on Coleman to *Time* magazine: "I immediately recognized it as religious metaphor. But it was dangerous language because of the ability to misinterpret it. I think it was more out of naivete than meanness").

In the same statement, Farrakhan called Hitler "a great man," and continued: "The Jews don't like Farrakhan, so they call me Hitler. Well, that's a good name. Hitler was a very great man. He wasn't great for me as a black person, but he was a great German. . . . He rose Germany up from nothing. Well, in a sense you could say there's a similarity in that we are rising our people up from nothing."

On "Meet the Press" on April 8, Jackson called Farrakhan's threat to Coleman "a bit inciting and distasteful," but refused to repudiate him personally—"I'm not going to do that. I don't think it's fair for you to attempt to make me do that."

The Republicans, encouraged by Jackson's problems, were gearing up to make a major appeal for the Jewish vote; campaign aides predicted Reagan would win 50 percent. The White House hired a new Jewish liaison, Marshall Breger. Vice President George Bush went on the attack, charging before the American Israel Public Affairs Committee that Jackson had not taken a firm stand against anti-

Semitism, adding, "I also cannot understand why Walter Mondale and Gary Hart have not continued to speak out loudly and clearly against this."

Mondale and Hart had, in fact, attacked Farrakhan's comments. When Jackson again talked about Farrakhan's "redemption" during the debate on the eve of the Texas primary, Mondale said, "I'm a preacher's kid, I believe in redemption, too. But that's going a little far, don't you think?" The remark was well taken—it pointed to several serious flaws in Jackson's use of theological language. For Christians, redemption comes from God, through Christ; people do not redeem themselves and they do not redeem other people. Of course, people do talk about "redemption" in everyday terms— "After striking out three times, he redeemed himself by driving in the winning run." But even in these terms, redemption implies an offense for which one must be redeemed. Similarly, Christian theology demands that in order to obtain forgiveness, a person must first acknowledge an offense and ask for forgiveness—in other words, repent. But Jackson offered Farrakhan an easy forgiveness; in the absence of Farrakhan's "repentance," Jackson had no right to "forgive" him in either theological or everyday language.

Jackson's continued refusal to dissociate himself from Farrakhan remained a major issue through May and June. The issue of "Black-Jewish tensions" continued to receive heavy media coverage, largely obscuring the fact that the black-Jewish political alliance remained intact. Black and Jewish members of congress pointed out that they had similar voting records; in particular, most black members supported aid to Israel and most Jewish members supported civil rights and opposed South Africa's apartheid. A *Washington Post*-ABC poll found that blacks supported Israel by a 3 to 1 margin over the Arab states, the same as the general population. And Jews had helped elect black mayors in Chicago and Philadelphia, where their percentage of support for Harold Washington and Wilson Goode was double that of other whites. In addition, 75 percent of the Jews in California had voted for Los Angeles Mayor Tom Bradley in his narrow loss in the 1982 governor's race.

There were some important efforts at smoothing over black-Jewish tensions, but some took a harder line than others. On May 31, Perlmutter told a national Antidefamation League (ADL) meeting that Jackson's rhetoric was "indistinguishable from that of anti-Semites." On May 3, Howard Friedman, president of the American Jewish Committee, told an AJC meeting in New York that "Jesse Jackson's candidacy has been laced by an attitude toward Jews which, if not anti-Semitic itself, is clearly not anti-anti-Semitic."

The issue finally exploded in late June, when it was reported that Farrakhan, in a radio broadcast, had called Judaism a "gutter religion." (Farrakhan later said that he had been misquoted—he said he had called it a "dirty religion," but a tape of the broadcast obtained by the *Chicago Tribune* supported the "gutter religion" version). Farrakhan also called supporters of Israel part of "a criminal conspiracy" and the creation of the State of Israel an "outlaw act." Mondale denounced Farrakhan's remarks as "venomous, bigoted, and obscene," but he stopped short of dissociating himself from Jackson, whose first reaction was to avoid comment. "I don't understand what he said," Jackson said from Cuba, where he had gone to meet with Fidel Castro. "I don't understand the context of it. I think it's absurd that you are trying to get a reaction from me on this. In America people have freedom of speech to say what they want about whom they want to. Don't keep putting me in the middle of that."

One of the strongest reactions came from Rabbi Alexander Schindler, president of the Union of American Hebrew Congregations, who attacked the silence of US political and religious leaders. "Where are the voices of conscience among the American people," he asked.

... In the past, one of the glories of the American democratic system has been that racial and religious groups vilified by bigotry were not forced to stand alone. ... They could always count on a coalition of decency to speak out not only in their defense, but in support of the values of racial brotherhood and religious understanding embedded in the history and tradition of the American democracy. Those voices appear to be silent today. That is reason for deep concern on the part of American Jews and of all Americans who cherish the moral courage that has ennobled our pluralistic society in the past.

The silence Schindler attacked was broken as he described it. Farrakhan's latest remarks seemed to be the "smoking gun" that gave church and civil rights groups the signal to speak out more forcefully. Claire Randall, general secretary of the National Council of Churches, said, "There is no place in this nation for the articulation of the kind of bigotry apparent in Mr. Farrakhan's statement about the Jewish faith. This unwarranted slur on an ancient and important religion is a threat to freedom of religion in this country." The Rev. Donald Heinstschel, associate general secretary of the National Conference of Catholic Bishops, said Farrakhan had "gone beyond the bounds of political rhetoric. We Catholics resist and denounce such pernicious characterizations of other religions." Benjamin Hooks, executive director of the NAACP, said his organization subscribed "to the tenets of the Judeo-Christian heritage and therefore cannot and will not be a party to casting aspersions on Judaism."

Finally, Jackson himself responded. "I am a Judeo-Christian," he said, "and the roots of my faith run deep in the Judeo-Christian tradition. Such statements have no place in my own theology or in this campaign. I will not permit Minister Farrakhan's words, wittingly or unwittingly, to divide the Democratic Party." Jackson said Farrakhan "is not a part of my campaign."

Despite Jackson's statement, the primary season ended with a widespread feeling of unease about how Jackson and other Democrats would handle the residue of the Farrakhan affair. Jackson continued to dominate both the religious and political life of the Democratic Party.

THE CONVENTIONS

Before the 1984 conventions began, Mondale had the Democratic nomination locked up. Then the focus shifted to his choice of a running mate. Most observers believed Mondale would not ask Hart to run with him; at the same time, there was mounting pressure from women's groups, armed with polls showing a significant "gender gap" of women favoring the Democrats, urging Mondale to pick a woman. Others pressed for a southerner, like Senator Lloyd Bentsen, a moderate Texan, or Dale Bumpers, an Arkansas liberal with a track record of winning in the suburbs.

Mondale talked with Bentsen, but from the beginning he said he was looking to make a symbolic statement with his choice of a vice presidential candidate. Many believe Mondale's first choice was New York Governor Mario Cuomo, the son of an Italian immigrant and an eloquent speaker who had emerged as both an effective spokesman for the New Deal wing of the party and a Reagan-like figure of optimism; but Cuomo ruled out the nomination, citing a pledge to serve a full term as governor. Mondale held widely publicized meetings with people he was considering: Los Angeles Mayor Tom Bradley, a black son of a sharecropper who had narrowly missed being elected governor of California in 1982; Henry Cisneros, the thirty-seven-year-old Hispanic mayor of San Antonio; Mayor Wilson Goode of Philadelphia, a black elected in 1982; Mayor Dianne Feinstein of San Francisco; and Representative Geraldine Ferraro, an Italian Catholic from "Archie Bunker's district" in Queens, chair of the Democratic Platform Committee, and a favorite of party leaders like House Speaker Tip O'Neill. The focus on women and minority candidates, including some with no real credentials for the vice presidency, coupled with an apparent slighting of southerners and white males, accentuated Mondale's image of catering to special interests—Bentsen joked, "I may be the last white male considered for the vice presidency."

Mondale received at least a temporary outpouring of good will when, before the convention began, he picked Ferraro—the first woman to appear on a major party ticket. Mondale tried to use Ferraro—as both a woman and the daughter of immigrants—as a symbol of opportunity in America. With the choice of Ferraro, the ticket also shifted into an emphasis on "values"—both candidates offered new and consistent references to family, faith, neighborhood, work, and patriotism, using the kind of rhetoric that had been coopted by the Republicans in recent elections. Mondale undid much of the good will he earned with the choice of Ferraro with an aborted effort to replace the chairman of the Democratic National Committee, Charles Mannatt, with Bert Lance, chairman of the Georgia Democratic Party and a controversial figure from the Carter Administration. Lance had resigned as Carter's budget director to deal with charges of illegal banking practices in Georgia. Although he was later acquitted of the charges, Lance was considered a political liability, even though the politically moderate born-again Christian was highly popular throughout the South. Mondale had picked Lance to reassure the South that he had not written it off after picking another northern liberal as his running mate, but when he was forced to drop Lance, he hurt himself with a constituency he needed to reach.

It was Ferraro, however, who introduced the first overtly religious issue in the campaign. She reacted angrily when a sign at her first campaign stop asked how she could be a good Catholic and still support legal abortion; she countered that Reagan "walks around calling himself a good Christian, but I don't for one minute believe it because the [his] policies are so terribly unfair." Ferraro's reaction came from the gut; it was natural for a Catholic raised on the *Baltimore Catechism* with its emphasis on the "corporal works of mercy" and the Sermon on the Mount—feed the hungry, clothe the naked. Her reaction typified the degree of animosity between politicians holding a conservative and liberal religious worldview. But the remark was a serious political mistake.

Mondale supported Ferraro, explaining, "My faith has taught me unmistakably that social justice is part of a Christian's responsibility. My upbringing taught me a sense of community . . . a sense of responsibility, one toward another. He [Reagan] would have to explain how he came to a different conclusion." Cuomo argued that religion was "a fair issue" because the Republicans had created the religion issue. But Senator John Glenn said, "There is one being who's sure of how good Christians we are, and it's not a mortal being. It's up to God." Dianne Feinstein, who is Jewish, said it was a "terrible mistake" for Ferraro to make religion an issue: "It comes back to haunt people. I don't think anybody's religion has anything to do with their ability to serve in government."

A Reagan press spokesman, John Buckley, said Reagan's "Christianity goes without saying. She should leave questions of this sort to a higher authority. Questions about any candidates commitment to religion should not be part of the political discourse." Reagan himself refused to comment directly on the Ferraro remark, but he emerged from a meeting of ethnic leaders marking Captive Nations Week saying, "I feel very good right now because there's a priest here who told me he thinks I'm a good Christian." The priest was Msgr. Stephen Chomko, president of the Fraternal Association of Ukranian Catholics in the United States and pastor of St. Michael's Church in Hartford, Connecticut.

Ferraro never quite apologized for the remark, but she did say that she had to think more before she spoke. She described her anger at having her own faith questioned: "I guess that gets to you. You kind of turn around and say, 'Don't do that to me. If you're going to do it, I'm not going to stand by and let you get away with it.' That I may have to control."

The conventions themselves reflected the same differences in religious style seen over the past few years. For the Democrats, religious influence was more subtle; it was a motivating force for political leaders, an encouragement for them to use government to do good. For the Republicans, religion was overt, with religious constituencies assiduously courted and religious issues narrowly defined.

There were no big name religious leaders praying at the Democratic convention in San Francisco. Mondale had asked an old friend, Archbishop John Roach of St. Paul-Minneapolis, a former president of the National Conference of Catholic Bishops who prayed at Carter's inauguration, to pray at the convention; but Roach declined, saying he did not want to appear partisan. Jerry Falwell and other New Right leaders sponsored a "Family Forum" before both party conventions; the Catholic Archdiocese of San Francisco's Commission on Social Justice said "the forum's sponsors include some notable personalities who have in the past supported dissemination of material that has fomented violence and injustice against lesbian-gay identified persons in the city of San Francisco."

The rhetoric of "values" pervaded the convention, particularly in the keynote address delivered by Cuomo, who offered several specific religious references: after charging Reagan with practicing "Social Darwinism," a survival-of-the-fittest mentality, he said, "We would rather have laws written by the patron of this great city, the man called 'the world's most sincere Democrat'—St. Francis of Assisi—than laws written by Darwin." Referring to the specter of a second Reagan term, Cuomo asked, "What kind of Supreme Court will we have? We must ask ourselves what kind of court and country will be fashioned by the man who believes in having government mandate people's religion and morality?" Cuomo cited Anglican Bishop Desmond Tutu of South Africa—who was later awarded the Nobel Peace Prize—as an example of a voice for human rights being ignored by the Reagan administration. And he hit hard at US support for the government of El Salvador—"We give money to Latin American governments that murder nuns, and then we lie about it."

The most overtly religious speech came from Jesse Jackson who, to the relief of party officials, was conciliatory—it was the "good" Jesse Jackson who spoke, opening by saying, "Tonight we come together bound by our faith in a mighty God." His speech was full of biblical references—"feed the hungry, clothe the naked. . . . There is a time to sow and a time to reap." He even quoted the Christian Right's favorite biblical passage, 2 Chronicles 7:14: "If my people, which are called by my name, shall humble themselves, and pray, and seek my face, and turn from their wicked ways; then will I hear from Heaven, and will forgive their sin, and will heal their land." Jackson's use of that passage brought home the degree to which political differences really were religious differences in 1984—Jesse Jackson and Jerry Falwell agreed that America had to repent for its "wicked ways," but were far from agreement as to just what those "wicked ways" were.

Democratic party officials squelched a proposed convention condemnation of anti-Semitism, but Jackson apologized to American Jews for his past remarks:

If in my low moments, in word, deed or attitude, through some error of temper, taste, or tone, I have caused anyone discomfort, created pain, or revived someone's fears, that was not my truest self. If there were occasions when my grape turned into a raisin and my joy bell lost its resonance, please forgive me. Charge it to my head and not to my heart. . . . I am not a perfect servant. I am a public servant, doing my best against the odds as I develop and serve.

Be patient, God is not finished with me yet. We are much too intelligent, much too bound by our Judeo-Christian heritage, much too victimized by racism, sexism, militarism, and anti-Semitism, much too threatened as historical scapegoats to go on divided from one another.

When Jackson's speech was over, the delegates clasped hands, swayed and sang hymns—just like at a Baptist church.

The Republican Convention was a Fundamentalist revival—punctuated by a few bows toward Catholics—from start to finish. Two religious flaps arose before the Convention even began. Hyman Bookbinder, Washington representative of the American Jewish Committee, learned that the host committee in Dallas planned to include a copy of the New Testament in the welcome kits of the five thousand delegates and alternates; he complained to a White House aide, and the Bibles were not included. Bookbinder said, "All this is part of a general effort to formally Christianize America, and that's not what our founding fathers wanted this country to be. I expect they will realize the possible political consequences."

The second incident involved a letter sent to priests and ministers across Texas the week before the convention. The letter, addressed "Dear Christian Leader" and signed by Senator Paul Laxalt of Nevada, chairman of the Reagan-Bush campaign committee, said: "As leaders under God's authority, we cannot afford to resign ourselves to idle neutrality in an election that will confirm or silence the President who has worked on your behalf and on behalf of all Americans." The letter spoke of Reagan's "unwavering commitment to the traditional values which I know you share" and concluded by asking the clergymen to "organize a voter registration campaign in your church . . . to help assure that those in your ministry will have a voice in the upcoming elections . . . a voice that will surely help secure the reelection of President Reagan and Vice President Bush." The letter was accompanied by a flyer marked "Christian Voter Program Information Enclosed" and a photograph of Reagan with the headline, "President Reagan Has Been Faithful in His Support of Issues of Concern to Christian Citizens."

Christian Right involvement in the convention was apparent in the clergy picked to pray at the opening and closing sessions. The invocation was given by televangelist James Robison, who had previously condemned Social Security as immoral and proclaimed that there would be no peace on Earth until the Second Coming of Christ. Robison said,

We pray, Father, for wisdom to all Americans that they may be able to discern between those who truly care for our well-being and those who speak well of our family while at the same time embracing and even encouraging practices and lifestyles which could lead to the diminishing value of our family and even the destruction of our families. . . . We pray that people will not look to government as the all provident one, as the provider, but rather in the proper sense of the word, as the protector of the rights, the freedom, the liberty of our people. . . . We thank you, Father, for the leadership of President Ronald Reagan. We ask that you continue to direct him. . . . We give our thanks in the name of Jesus Christ, Our Lord and Savior. Amen.

Jerry Falwell delivered the Convention benediction:

It is a great honor to ask our Lord's blessing upon a man that many of us believe, indeed, to be our greatest president since Lincoln and an equally prestigious and honorable vice president who have been God's instrument in rebuilding America. . . . We thank you for a president that has led us in such a way that we have hope for our children to grow up in freedom, to know what it means to be free born and to enjoy the privileges of being Americans as we have. . . . We pray this prayer in Jesus' name. Amen.

In between, prayers were offered by two Catholic bishops—John Cardinal Krol of Philadelphia, a friend of Republican presidential candidates since Richard Nixon, and Rene Gracida of Corpus Christi. Gracida said his benediction would be "nothing more and nothing less than asking God's blessing upon our system of government," not a plea for God to bless one political party. "I would have accepted an invitation from the Democratic Party and done the same thing," he said. "I am a registered Democrat and have been all of my life."

During an address before the convention, Laxalt referred to Cuomo's recent disagreements with Archbishop John O'Connor of New York. O'Connor had said at a press conference in June, "I don't see how a Catholic in good conscience can vote for a candidate who explicitly supports abortion." Cuomo challenged the clear implication that Catholics could only vote for right-to-life candidates. O'Connor backed off, saying, "It is neither my responsibility nor my desire to evaluate the qualifications of any individuals or any political party for any public office, or of any individuals holding office." Referring to the dispute, Laxalt, a Catholic, thundered, "Shame on you, Mario Cuomo."

Reagan himself offered the most controversial comments of the week in an address to seventeen thousand people attending a nondenominational prayer breakfast held on the last day of the Convention.

Today there are those who are fighting to make sure that voluntary prayer is not returned to the classrooms. And the frustrating thing for the great majority of Americans who support and understand the special importance of religion in the national life, the frustrating thing is that those who are attacking religion claim they are doing it in the name of tolerance, freedom, and open-mindedness. Question: Isn't the real truth that they are intolerant of religion? They refuse to tolerate its importance in our lives. . . .

The truth is, politics and morality are inseparable. And as morality's foundation is religion, religion and politics are necessarily related. We need religion as a guide. We need it because we are imperfect. And our government needs the church because only those humble enough to admit they're sinners can bring to democracy the tolerance it requires in order to survive.

A state is nothing more than a reflection of its citizens. The more decent the citizens, the more decent the state. If you practice a religion, whether you're Catholic, Protestant, Jewish, or guided by some other faith, then your private life will be influenced by a sense of moral obligation. And so, too, will your public life. One affects the other. . . .

We established no religion in this country, nor will we ever. We command no worship. We mandate no belief. But we poison our society when we remove its theological underpinnings. We court corruption when we leave it bereft of belief.

At the convention's close, *Washington Post* reporter James Dickenson wrote from Dallas, "Religion was as powerful an influence at the Republican National Convention here this week as the traditional secular themes of tax cuts and a strong national defense."

THE CAMPAIGN

The furor caused by the political use of religion at the Republican Convention provided Mondale with a major campaign issue, and, with the encouragement of party leaders, he promised to address it.

The first opportunity came when both he and Reagan addressed the International Convention of B'nai B'rith in Washington on September 6, 1984. Mondale criticized the voting record issued by the Religious Right group Christian Voice, Jerry Falwell, and Jimmy Swaggart by name. He also spoke from his own experience:

> My dad was a minister. My mom was a director of religious education. My wife Joan's dad was a minister. I was taught to believe in the God of the Old and New Testaments—a God of justice, of mercy, and of love. I was taught that we bear witness to our faith through a life of commitment, consideration, and service to our fellow men and women. In learning my own faith, I was taught to respect the faith of others.
>
> . . . What I am doing today is something that, in twenty-five years of public life, I never thought I would do: I have never before had to defend my faith in a political campaign. I have never thought it proper for political leaders to use religion to partisan advantage by advertising their own faith and questioning their opponent's.
>
> I believe in an America that honors what Thomas Jefferson first called the "wall of separation between church and state." That freedom has made our faith unadulterated and unintimidated. It had made Americans the most religious people on earth. Today, the religion clauses of the First Amendment do not need to be fixed; they need to be followed.
>
> I believe in an America where government is not permitted to dictate the religious life of our people; where religion is a private matter between individuals and God, between families and their churches and synagogues, with no room for politicians in between. I do not for one moment claim a partisan monopoly on the beliefs I have just outlined. They are the common heritage of all Americans: Protestants, Catholics and Jews; Democrats and Republicans—everyone.

Mondale did a good job of addressing religious liberty issues by, in effect, defending the First Amendment's "no establishment" clause. But he gave half a speech; what was missing was a positive vision of the way in which religious leaders and citizens with religious concerns *could* participate in the public debate.

For his part, Reagan devoted only a small portion of his speech to church-state issues, but it was an effective few words:

> The United States is, and must remain, a nation of openness to people of all beliefs. Our very unity has been strengthened by this pluralism. That's how we began. This is how we must always be. The ideals of our country leave no

room whatsoever for intolerance, anti-Semitism, or bigotry of any kind—none. The unique thing about America is a wall in our Constitution, separating church and state. It guarantees there will never be a state religion in this land, but at the same time it makes sure that every single American is free to choose and practice his or her religious beliefs or to choose no religion at all. Their rights shall not be questioned or violated by the state.

This was the only time in Ronald Reagan's presidency, perhaps in his career, that he had referred to the "wall of separation" between church and state; the phrase served like magic to reassure most Americans that, despite the convention rhetoric, Reagan did respect religious freedom. Reagan kept an intentionally low profile on religious issues throughout most of the campaign, and Mondale's efforts to use the issue against Reagan—including TV ads linking Reagan to Jerry Falwell—never took hold. In a sense, Mondale won the battle, but lost the war: public opinion was so strongly on his side that Reagan simply capitulated, walking away from the issue just the way he walked away from his original support for Bob Jones University in its dispute with the Internal Revenue Service. In the process, he successfully defused the issue for the rest of the campaign.

ARMAGEDDON THEOLOGY

Reagan, however, did raise another religious issue which posed a temporary threat to his reelection. Or, rather, an issue he had raised in the past came back to haunt him—a fascination with Armageddon theology, the biblical foretelling of the end of the world. In separate research, journalist Ronnie Dugger and the Christic Institute, a liberal Washington think tank, unearthed a number of comments Reagan had made over the years about Armageddon:

- In 1981, Reagan discussed Armageddon with Senator Howell Heflin (D-Alabama) and said, "Russia is going to get involved in it."
- The same year, Falwell told *The Los Angeles Times* that Reagan told him, "Jerry, I sometimes believe we're heading very fast for Armageddon right now."
- In October 1983, Reagan told Tom Dine of the American-Israel Public Affairs Committee: "You know, I turn back to your ancient prophets in the Old Testament and the signs foretelling Armaged-

don, and I find myself wondering if—if we're the generation that's going to see that come about. I don't know if you've noted any of those prophecies lately, but, believe me, they certainly describe the times we're going through."

- In the December 6, 1983, *People* magazine, Reagan said, ". . . theologians have been studying the ancient prophecies—what would portend the coming of Armageddon?—and have said that never, in the time between the prophecies up until now, has there ever been a time in which so many of the prophecies are coming together. There have been times in the past when people thought the end of the world was coming, but never anything like this."

It was legitimate to be concerned with the question of whether or not Reagan believed in Armageddon theology because such a belief has a public, not merely a private, dimension. It is also the theological base upon which the political agenda of the Religious Right is built. For example, Jerry Falwell told the *Los Angeles Times*, "I think we're coming to an impasse. All of history is reaching a climax and . . . I do not think we have fifty years left. I don't think my children will live their full lives out, as I probably will." Jimmy Swaggart said in a November 1984 broadcast, "Jesus Christ is about to come back to catch his people away. You can almost hear the roar of Armageddon. The world is headed toward judgment." Tim LaHaye was even more self-confident, writing in *The Beginning of the End*, "There is no question that we are living in the last days."

The chief popularizer of Armageddon theology is Hal Lindsey, who spelled out his prophecy of the endtimes in his 1970 book *The Late Great Planet Earth* and a series of follow-ups. Armageddon theology is primarily based on interpretation of the Books of Daniel and Ezekiel in the Old Testament and the Book of Revelation in the New Testament. It says the events leading up to the coming of the Antichrist and the Second Coming can be foretold by the fulfillment of a series of signs.

Many of those signs—an increase of "wars and rumors of wars," extreme materialism, lawlessness, overpopulation, increase in speed and knowledge, departure from the Christian faith, and intensive demonic activity—have been found by Fundamentalists in past times.

Others are tied to fairly recent developments, including the growth of Soviet power and the Christian ecumenical movement. Falwell cites the work of the World Council of Churches, the National Council of Churches, and Vatican II as signs of a "unification of world systems" that mark the beginning of the end.

Beyond doubt, however, the most important "signs" in Armageddon theology involve the birth of the State of Israel in 1948. The return of Jews to Israel from all over the world was to many Fundamentalists the fulfillment of a key biblical prophecy—with the creation of Israel, Lindsey says, "the prophetic countdown began!" Lindsey and his followers believe the countdown sped up in 1967 when, as a result of the Arab-Israeli war, Israel regained control of Jerusalem.

Armageddon Theology as described by Lindsey, Falwell, and others offers a detailed outline of future events:

The first indication the end is coming will be "the Rapture," when Jesus will "catch up" those who believe in him and spirit them away. The next event is the beginning of a seven year period of "Tribulation," which will begin with the invasion of Israel by Russia, with help from Iran, Germany, and some African nations, perhaps Libya. (Some Fundamentalists believe the Rapture will occur during the Tribulation). According to Armageddon theology, Israel will receive help from a ten-nation European consortium (Pat Robertson is sure this is the Common Market) and in the ensuing chaos—in which China and India will invade Israel from the east—God will destroy Russia, killing five out of six soldiers, and preserve Israel. All will not stay well for Israel, however, as the head of the European Consortium will turn out to be the Antichrist, who will himself invade Israel, enter the rebuilt Temple in Jerusalem, and demand veneration. Israel will resist, and Christ will return with an army of raptured saints to defeat the Antichrist at Armageddon.

During all this, the vast majority of Israeli Jews will be killed, but the survivors will accept Christ. Falwell explains in *Nuclear War and the Second Coming of Jesus Christ* (1983), "The final purpose of the Tribulation will be to purge Israel. As gold is purified through the heat of the fire, so the nation of Israel will come through the Tribulation fit for the master's use." With all this complete, Christ will usher in the Millennium—one thousand years of peace until the final judgement and the creation of a "new Heaven and a new Earth."

Armageddon theology is actually a direct descendent of the biblical prophecy movement which began in the United States in the early nineteenth century. In the late nineteenth century, American Fundamentalists like Dwight L. Moody adopted the views of an Englishman, James Nelson Darby (1800–1882), who developed the theory of "dispensational premillennialism": "dispensational" referred to the division of time into seven periods, or dispensations; "premillennial" referred to the belief that Christ would return before one thousand years of peace.

In contrast, Catholic and mainline Protestant churches view Ezekiel, Daniel, and Revelation as examples of "apocalyptic" literature which must be understood as heavily symbolic commentaries on events at the times they were written. Most Evangelicals reject dispensationalism; not all Fundamentalists are dispensationalists; and not even all dispensationalists subscribe to Armageddon theology's emphasis on nuclear war.

The greatest danger posed by Armageddon theology is clearly to the pursuit of peace. One of the starkest attacks on peace comes from James Robison, who declares, "There'll be no peace until Jesus comes. That's what the Antichrist promises. Any preaching of peace prior to his return is heresy; it's against the word of God; it's Antichrist."

Armageddon theology's contempt for peace is particularly acute where the Middle East is concerned. The Camp David Peace Accords were an inspiration because they involved three men of different faiths—Jimmy Carter, a Christian; Menachem Begin, a Jew; and Anwar Sadat, a Muslim—each of whom drew on his religion's call for peace and love of neighbor to fashion a dramatic step toward peace. But Jerry Falwell mocked the Camp David accords: "You and I know that there's not going to be any real peace in the Middle East until one day the Lord Jesus Christ sits down upon the throne of David in Jerusalem."

An added concern about Armageddon theology's fatalism about war is its identification of the Soviet Union with the forces of evil and the United States with the forces of good. Such a worldview implies the futility, even the danger, of US-Soviet negotiations. That's one reason so many religious leaders were so upset by President Reagan's characterization of the Soviet Union as the "focus of evil in the modern world." And the president is not the only major figure involved in war-and-peace issues to use the rhetoric of Armageddon: Defense Secretary Caspar Weinberger responded to a Harvard student who asked if he believed the world would end by saying, "I have read the Book of Revelation"; Admiral James Watkins, chief of naval operations, blamed the death of 241 US servicemen in the 1983 Beirut bombing on the "forces of the Anti-Christ." And Hal Lindsey claims to have lectured at the Pentagon.

It was not surprising, particularly in light of the recent high priority given Reagan's religious beliefs, the question of his belief in Armageddon theology was fair game. The relevance of these comments coming from a sitting president of the United States was obvious: if he were convinced that biblical prophecies of the end of the world were being fulfilled, would he be inclined to help them along? In the first presidential debate, Marvin Kalb asked Reagan whether his belief in the coming of Armageddon affected his decision making.

Reagan replied:

> I think that what has been hailed as something that I'm supposedly as president discussing in principle is the result just of some philosophical discussions with people who are interested in the same things, and that is, the prophecies down through the years, the biblical prophecies of what would portend the coming of Armageddon, and so forth. And the fact that a number of theologians for the last decade or more have believed that this was true, that the prophecies are coming together that portend that. But no one knows whether Armageddon, those prophecies, mean that Armageddon is a thousand years away or the day after tomorrow. So I have never seriously warned and said we must plan according to Armageddon.

As Reagan began his answer, First Lady Nancy Reagan reportedly exclaimed, "Oh, no!" but, once again, Reagan was able to defuse a potentially damaging religious issue.

THE RELIGIOUS RIGHT

But if Reagan himself was relatively quiet on religion and politics issues throughout the balance of the campaign, others were not. The

1984 elections offer a case study of the way the Religious Right operates. There are several main elements in a Religious Right operation: voter registration focused on Fundamentalist churches; a high media profile, led by prominent televangelists; organized participation in political caucuses; targeting of vulnerable seats, and distribution of voting records portraying the "biblical" positions on issues.

A voting scorecard compiled by Christian Voice was used against congressional candidates all across the country. The major piece of the Religious Right's 1984 campaign was a forty-page magazine, the *Presidential Biblical Scoreboard*. The *Scoreboard*'s introduction, written by David Balsinger and Christian Voice leader Colonel V. Donner, said, "If you fail to vote conscientiously for godly rule, evil will continue to increase in our nation, as we have witnessed over the past few decades. Although most political candidates claim a Judeo-Christian heritage, it's important to carefully examine their actual position on the biblical-family-moral issues. . . . By using our *Scoreboard* and voting for candidates who support Judeo-Christian values, you will be doing your Christian duty in helping to reclaim America for God."

The *Scoreboard* had a clear Republican bias which operated by putting the best possible light on Reagan-Bush positions and the worst possible light on Mondale-Ferraro positions. For example, it listed Mondale's religion as "Humanist/Presbyterian," and quoted atheist Madalyn Murray O'Hair's description of Mondale as "an undercover atheist." The *Scoreboard* attempted a smear of Ferraro: after conceding that she had voted for the Child Protection Act of 1984, designed to curb production and distribution of child pornography, it said, "Meanwhile, investigative reporters determined in August that Ms. Ferraro is secretary-treasurer of her husband's management corporation which is part owner of a lower Manhattan building that houses a major national Mafia-run distributor of hard-core pornography." Ferraro's husband, John Zacarro, had no knowledge of his tenant's business and said he would not renew their lease when he found out; the *Scoreboard*'s implication of hypocrisy and an ethnic slur were clear.

Christian Voice claims to have distributed more than 5 million copies of the *Presidential Biblical Scorboard*. The *Scoreboard* was also distributed through the American Coalition for Traditional Values (ACTV), which represented the major Fundamentalist preachers and televangelists, including Jerry Falwell, Jimmy Swaggart, Pat Robertson, James Robison, and others. It was headed by Tim La-Haye, who charged that, "The problem with America is . . . we do not have enough of God's ministers running the country."

(The ACTV agenda included a new proposal—quotas in government for Fundamentalists. One of "the six main ACTV objectives" was "The Talent Bank: A vigorous attempt will be made to find (through our network) qualified Christians to receive positions in government as follows: a) Appointive offices—3,000 positions. b) Civil Service Employment—3,310,000 positions.")

The televangelists who made up the backbone of ACTV devoted considerable activity on their own programs in the fall to urging their viewers to vote for the right candidates. Pat Robertson said on October 4, 1984, "We're asking for godly people to be in office. We're praying particularly in this election you want men of God in various levels of life . . . men and women who love God, who believe in the Bible, who have a principle, who are men and women of integrity and honesty and decency. These are the kind of people we want in office." On October 17 Robertson asked, "Is America going to allow the 4 percent of the people who claim to be atheists to strip away the theocratic, theist beliefs of the 96 percent of the people who are believers? . . . No society can make its public policy hostage to the will of non-believers and allow a few courts and a few judges to twist the will of the majority."

Falwell earlier argued (on September 23) that, "This Bible is God's law and it's the basis for Constitutional law and the Judeo-Christian ethic upon which this country was established." On November 4 he said,

I'm convinced that this election is the most serious election, perhaps in the history of our country. I'm convinced that we're either going to stand up for the principles that God can honor and bless, put an end to the murder of the unborn, stand up against every moral cancer in our society; stand up for strong national defense and leadership that will lead us on to peace for our children and our children's children, or we are going to lose the freedoms and privileges that we have known for so long in this country. . . . We see how Satan rises up those who have a secularistic philosophy to oppose those who like us have a Judeo-Christian philosophy.

Falwell and others also spoke of their personal contact with Reagan and White House advisors; Reagan met with a group of ACTV leaders. Falwell said on June 24, 1984, "I met with the president last Friday. We were talking about Central America. There were a number of us there discussing the issue of Nicaragua and El Salvador." On July 29 Swaggart said, "Next week, I with other ministers of the Gospel will meet with the president and several of his advisors to try to find a way to stem the tide of evil."

ACTV and Christian Voice targeted congressional and local races in several states. The most noteworthy was Texas, where Christian Voice's "Texas Plan" was designed to serve as a model for future elections. Ray Allan, president of the American Christian Voice Foundation, led five thousand volunteers who distributed two-and-a-half million report cards on presidential and congressional candidates. Fundamentalist activists swamped Republican Party caucuses and by some estimates accounted for about one in six delegates to the state Republican convention. Christian Voice claims that 400,000 newly registered voters were registered by Fundamentalists. Christian Voice targeted the open Senate seat and eight congressional seats in Texas; their senatorial candidate and four of their congressional candidates won. Joe Barton traveled with a Christian Voice pastor as an advisor and Richard Armey said at least 250 Christian activists worked in his campaign. During the campaign, successful Senate candidate Phil Gramm declared, "Our freedom does not come from the government of the US—it comes from God. And those who want freedom from religion are in the wrong country."

The Religious Right's activities took on a particularly ominous tone when "Christian" campaigns were waged against Jewish candidates:

- In Georgia, Republican Pat Swindall emphasized his Evangelical Christianity in his successful challenge of Democrat Elliott Levitas. A Baptist minister sent out a campaign letter asking support for Swindall because he was a "godly candidate." One church prayed for a specific number of votes for Swindall (115,000) and prayed that "Pat's opponent, Mr. Levitas, would come to know the Lord."

- In Michigan, Republican Congressman Mark Siljander and two state senators sent out a letter opposing Democrat Harold Wolpe: "As elected officials serving under the authority of Our Lord Jesus Christ, we felt it our responsibility to contact you before the November general election. . . . All of us, as born-again Evangelicals, feel it is our responsibility to share with you this election that we are vitally concerned about. . . . I am dismayed because [Wolpe] has voted against the traditional American values which have helped build this country into the Evangelistic arm it has become. . . . You can make the difference in helping send another Christian to Congress." Wolpe was reelected. (Siljander also signed a letter from Christian Voice urging pastors across the country to send bulk qualities of the *Scoreboard* to every church in their congressional district.)

- In California, supporters of Republican Rob Scribner distributed a flyer attacking Representative Mel Levine, saying Scribner's election would "restore America's moral foundation" and righteousness. A chart called "The Bible and Mel Levine" contrasted Levine's positions with alleged biblical ones. Levine was reelected.

THE BISHOPS AND ABORTION

The Religious Right was not the only major source of debate about "mixing religion and politics" in 1984. The nation's Catholic bishops returned to the center of a debate they had helped ignite eight years earlier.

In 1976, the first presidential election year following the US Supreme Court's decisions legalizing most abortions, the bishops had become involved in a major political dispute when a five-member committee met with the presidential candidates and declared that they were "encouraged" by President Ford's support for a constitutional amendment to limit abortion and "disappointed" in Jimmy Carter's opposition. While the bishops had made other comments, those remarks were widely interpreted as an endorsement of Ford until the National Conference of Catholic Bishops' Administrative Committee issued a statement reaffirming its position of not endorsing or opposing candidates or parties and urging Catholics to study a wide range of issues and vote their conscience.

Burned by their handling of the 1976 elections, the bishops held a very low profile in 1980. In 1983, the bishops issued a historic pastoral letter, *The Challenge of Peace,* addressed to questions of nuclear war and peace. The pastoral, which became the focus of national debate as the Reagan administration sought unsuccessfully to weaken its criticism of US policy, served the practical purpose of raising arms control to a parallel level to abortion in the bishops' political priorities.

In early 1984, the bishops released an updated version of a statement on "political responsibility" which again urged Catholics to study the issues and vote their conscience. But they were dragged into a national controversy when Archbishop John O'Connor of New York said, "I don't see how a Catholic in good conscience can vote for a candidate who explicitly supports abortion." O'Connor later met for an hour with New York governor Mario Cuomo, an obvious target of his remark, and said he would not attempt to tell Catholics how to vote.

On August 9, the president of the bishops' conference, Bishop James Malone of Youngstown, Ohio, issued a statement which conference spokesmen said was sparked by recent events, including Reagan's partisan appeals to religion; O'Connor's dispute with Cuomo; Ferraro's "good Christian" comment and her use of the argument that she was "personally opposed" to abortion, but would not let her personal religious beliefs affect her political decisions; and O'Connor's dispute with Cuomo.

Malone repeated that the bishops' conference "does not take positions for or against political candidates." In language obviously directed at Reagan, he said, "It would be regrettable if religion as such were injected into a political campaign through appeals to candidates' religious affiliations and commitments."

In language clearly directed at Ferraro, he said,

We reject the idea that candidates satisfy the requirements of rational analysis by saying their personal views should not influence their policy decisions;

the implied dichotomy—between personal morality and public policy—is simply not logically tenable in any adequate view of both. This position would be as unacceptable as would be the approach of a candidate or office-holder who pointed to his or her personal commitments as qualifications for public office, without proposing to take practical steps to translate these into policies or practical programs.

The Malone statement was an effort at being even-handed and it helped calm the waters, but only for a few weeks. On September 4, 1984, Archbishop Bernard Law of Boston, joined by seventeen other New England bishops, issued a statement defining abortion as "the critical issue of the moment." The statement said, "While nuclear holocaust is a future possibility, the holocaust of abortion is a present reality."

A few days later, O'Connor jumped back into the headlines. After his meeting with Cuomo, he had said he would speak out if he found a candidate had misrepresented Catholic teaching; now he had found one—Geraldine Ferraro. O'Connor had obtained a letter Ferraro had signed inviting fellow members of Congress to a briefing sponsored by Catholics for a Free Choice in September, 1982. In the letter, Ferraro had said that the Catholic position on abortion was "not monolithic." O'Connor charged that this misrepresented church teaching. At first, Ferraro did not know what O'Connor was talking about, but when she was reminded about the letter, she countered that she was not talking about the church's position, but about the position of American Catholics.

Ferraro was also strongly criticized by Bishop Joseph Timlin of Scranton; Timlin had been O'Connor's auxiliary bishop when he was bishop of Scranton before his appointment to New York. During the campaign, John Cardinal Krol of Philadelphia, Bishop Edward Head of Buffalo, and Archbishop Peter Gerety of Newark made friendly appearances with Reagan.

On September 13, Cuomo delivered a major speech at the University of Notre Dame in which he addressed the abortion issue within a broad political context. He defended his position on several levels: he argued that in a pluralistic society, Catholics could not impose their religious beliefs on others; he conceded that abortion was also a moral issue apart from Catholic teaching, but he argued that even if one agreed with the moral principle that abortion was wrong, such agreement did not dictate the best political response; he argued that an abortion ban was not practical or enforceable. Finally, he turned the tables and in effect blamed the church for not being able to convince its own people to refrain from having abortions. "We seem to be in the position," he said, "of asking government to make criminal what we believe to be sinful because we ourselves can't stop committing the sin."

A number of bishops rejected Cuomo's argument without refuting it; that is, none denied his claim that there was not a sufficient public consensus to ban abortion. Instead, some bishops pressured Cuomo to help build that consensus. O'Connor said, "You have to *uphold* the law, the Constitution says. It does not say that you must *agree* with the law, or that you cannot work to change the law."

Bishop Malone issued another statement of October 14, again making clear that, "We do not seek the formation of a voting bloc nor do we preempt the right and duty of individuals to decide conscientiously whom they will support for public office. Rather, having stated our positions, we encourage members of our own church and all citizens to examine the positions of candidates on issues and decide who will best contribute to the common good of society."

Without mentioning Cuomo, Malone both conceded his point and urged him to help shape an antiabortion consensus.

We realize that citizens and public officials may agree with our moral arguments while disagreeing with us and among themselves on the legal and policy steps to take. . . . The prudential judgment that political solutions are not now feasible does not justify failure to undertake the effort. Whether the issue be the control, reduction and elimination of nuclear arms or the legal protection of the unborn, the task is to work for the feasibility of what may now be deemed unfeasible.

The Malone statement did not resolve the issue. On October 22, 1984,twenty-three bishops, led by Auxiliary Bishop Thomas Gumbleton of Detroit, issued a statement taking on Law and O'Connor.

To claim that nuclear was is only a potential evil and that abortion is actual neglects a terrible reality. For indeed, there can be no possibility of exercising moral responsibility against nuclear war if we wait until the missiles have been released. Now is the time . . . to take a position on this moral issue. For right now we possess in our hands the means for the annihilation of the human race.

Many Catholics were waiting for some word from the most influential bishop in the country, Joseph Cardinal Bernardin of Chicago. Bernardin had chaired the committee which drafted the bishops' peace pastoral and was now chairman of the bishops Ad Hoc Committee for Pro-Life Activities. In that role, he had developed the image of the "seamless garment," or the "consistent ethic of life" which linked together a host of issues—including abortion, peace, poverty, civil rights, and opposition to US policies in Central America—into one package. The "seamless garment" was the most systematic challenge to the "single issue" approach in which abortion was the determining issue.

Bernardin spoke at the Woodstock Theological Center at Georgetown University on October 25. Bernardin's talk could not influence the outcome of the election—Reagan was now ahead by a wide margin in the polls— but it set the terms for the religion and politics debate within Catholic circles after the election.

At Georgetown, Bernardin defended the "consistent ethic" approach: "The value of the framework of a consistent ethic is that it forces us to face the full range of threats to life. It resists a 'one-issue' focus by the church, even when the urgent issue is abortion or nuclear arms."

Bernardin also implicitly rejected Law's argument: "The policy of abortion on demand needs to be resisted and reversed," he said. "But this does not mean the nuclear question can be ignored or relegated to a subordinate basis. The only 'cure' for the nuclear threat is to prevent any use of nuclear weapons. We are not confronting a hypothetical or speculative future danger. The possibility of a nuclear war is a clear and present danger."

Finally, Bernardin endorsed Malone's most recent statement. "Clearly we do want people in public office whose deepest beliefs shape their character and determine the quality of their leadership. We choose public officials in part because we hope they will infuse public life with certain convictions. However, relating convictions to policy choices is a complex process. But it is precisely that complexity which should be debated."

WHAT HAPPENED IN 1984

The mixing of religion and politics was not a hypothetical issue in 1984: The average political reporter covering the elections had to cover the influence of religion in shaping the personalities and worldviews of the major presidential candidates, anti-Semitism, the complexities of the Protestant Fundamentalist movement, church-state law, Catholic theology, in fighting among Black Muslims, and biblical prophesy.

The 1984 election has to be analyzed in two stages—the presidential level and the congressional level. At the presidential level, the election represented a sweeping victory for a personally popular president in a time of peace and prosperity; given those considerations, a Democratic win would have been a major upset. William Schneider, a public opinion expert based at the American Enterprise Institute, pointed out in *The New Republic,* "The polls make it clear that if Ronald Reagan had run for re-election under the conditions prevailing in 1982 instead of 1984, he would have lost decisively, all his charm and amiability notwithstanding." But he didn't, and he didn't.

At the same time, Mondale had a serious image problem. He proposed raising taxes, always an unpopular gambit. His campaign also seemed to confirm his "wimp" image, reflected in the fact that he received the support of only 31 percent of white males. This reflected two factors: first, by spending so much time trying to resolve the differences between blacks and Jews, Mondale projected the impression that those were the only groups whose votes he wanted; second, by failing to stand up to Jackson at key points during the primaries and by appearing to give in to pressure from women's groups in picking Ferraro, he raised doubts about his political backbone.

For all his problems, however, Mondale did leave a legacy on which future Democratic presidential candidates may build. He successfully recaptured the rhetoric of "work, family, neighborhood, and church" for the Democrats. He also mobilized public opinion against the partisan use of religion. While the Religious Right was helped by Reagan's victory—anyone in a winning coalition usually is—there is no reason to view that victory as a mandate for the Religious Right itself. In fact, the Religious Right suffered a major defeat in the presidential race. "Religion and politics" was the only spontaneous issue that broke in Mondale's favor during the campaign. The orgy of Fundamentalism at the Republican National Convention, particularly Reagan's remarks at the Dallas prayer breakfast, created a firestorm of concern—so much so, in fact, that Reagan surrendered, neutralizing the issue just as he had become the candidate of arms control and Social Security. Reagan's use of the "wall of separation between church and state" metaphor and a general cooling of his religious rhetoric during the campaign and his "nice guy" image convinced Americans that he was not a religious fanatic—giving Mondale a pyrrhic victory.

For his part, Reagan's most impressive feat was winning some 80 percent of the votes of white born-again Christians and bringing them into the Republican Party in large numbers. Reagan's vote total alone, however, is misleading; it is about the same as Nixon's in 1972, when there was no organized Religious Right. What is particularly impressive is a poll conducted by the Committee for the Study of the American Electorate which found that born-again white Protestants made up 28 percent of new voters as opposed to 20 percent of all voters and split 77 to 18 for Reagan, with 58 percent identifying themselves as Republicans and 30 percent as Democrats.

Despite this, however, it would be inaccurate to identify all white born-again Protestants with the Religious Right. A CBS-*New York Times* poll found that only 18 percent of that group cited abortion as one of the two top issues which influenced their vote, and only a quarter cited Reagan's support for "traditional values." The poll found that 49 percent of white born-again Protestants cited arms control and defense as one of the two most important issues affecting their vote; 43 percent cited the economy; 20 percent cited the federal deficit; and 14 percent cited fairness to the poor. Among those citing abortion as a factor, 93 percent voted for Reagan. Abortion and "traditional values" were less influential than Reagan's personality and record in the voting of white Evangelicals.

White born-again Protestants were more likely than Catholics (8 percent) and other white Protestants (4 percent) to cite abortion as a major factor in determining their vote. As large as this figure is, however, it means that only one white Evangelical in five considered abortion a voting issue—which means that four in five did not. This figure itself is at odds with the impression created by Religious Right leaders that virtually all white Evangelicals are motivated by the abortion issue. Similarly, about one in four white born-again Protestants cited Reagan's appeal to "traditional values" as a reason for their vote, a significant figure, but, again, considerably less than 100 percent.

Reagan received a record 56 percent of the Catholic vote, but the prolonged internal church debate over abortion was not a major factor. As noted, the CBS-*New York Times* poll found that only 8 percent of white Catholics cited abortion as one of the top two issues affecting their vote. (Within this group, 71 percent voted for Reagan, 28 percent for Mondale). But 18 percent of Catholics—twice as many as those citing abortion—cited fairness to the poor as a factor in determining their vote, and this group favored Mondale by 79 to 20 percent. The most frequently cited issues among white Catholics were arms control and defense (53 percent), the economy (41 percent), and the federal deficit (24 percent).

In congressional races, the Religious Right had its share of both wins and losses, but its own self-congratulatory analysis is suspect because it acts as though the "religious issues" were the only factor in the election, ignoring Reagan's Dr. Feelgood impact on the American people and an apparently booming economy. For example, the Religious Right's major victory was the reelection of its hero, Jesse Helms, but even here, the Reagan coattails were an important factor.

ACTV claims it made the difference in the shift of four congressional seats in Texas, three in North Carolina and one in Georgia. It was certainly a factor, but the races deserve a closer look. *The Almanac of American Politics,* respected for its objective analysis by left, right, and center, saw only two of those seats as "safe" for their Democratic incumbents in 1984—even though it described one, Representative Elliot Levitas's district in suburban Atlanta, as basically Republican in make-up. The *Almanac* predicted trouble for the three North Carolina Democrats elected in 1982, when the Democrats picked up twenty-six seats nationally: Ike Andrews in the 4th District; Charles Robin Britt in the 6th; and James McClure Clarke (who won by 1 percent in 1982) in the 11th. In Texas, the Almanac saw "tough" races in the 14th District for Bill Patman and in the 26th for Tom Vandergriff, who won by 344 votes in 1982 in a newly created district that was widely expected to go Republican. The Republicans also picked up the seat vacated by Kent Hance, who quit to run in the senatorial primaries; here, the *Almanac* said, "essentially this is a Republican district."

Of more long-term importance were gains made by the Religious Right at the state level. Working with pro-life groups, it took over about half of the Republican-Independent Party in Minnesota. It also claimed to have taken over the Republican party apparatus in Texas, where right-wingers scored victories in local as well as congressional races; Religious Right leaders said most of the 400,000 newly registered Republicans were "Christians." ACTV leaders said most of the 400,000 newly registered Republicans were "Christians." ACTV leaders said they would export the "Texas plan"—basically, heavy volunteer organizing—to other states in coming elections. But the Religious Right has captured and then lost the Republican Party apparatus in Alaska and Oregon; it has yet to prove durable.

The Religious Right's losses were also significant in 1984. The other Religious Right senator up for reelection, Roger Jepsen of Iowa, lost to populist Tom Harkin. Ron Godwin of the Moral Majority blames Jepsen's defeat on his failure to seek highly visible, organized Religious Right support; but poor economic conditions in Iowa made this a Democratic year—Mondale lost by 8 points in Iowa as opposed to 18 points nationally. The Religious Right also lost four other races where it devoted a great deal of effort—Albert Lee Smith against Senator Howell Heflin in Alabama; Ed Bethune against Senator David Pryor in Arkansas; Jack Lousma against Senator Carl Levin in Michigan; and John Paul Stark against Representative George Brown in California.

A case can be made that the Religious Right is primarily a southern phenomenon that will have its greatest impact when economic times are good. But the movement's impact has become more diffuse. In 1978 and 1980, it hurt liberal Democrats; in 1982, when a recession led to a Democratic year, it didn't hurt anyone; in 1984, it hurt conservative Democrats and moderate Republicans.

A final question is what the 1984 election did to further the national debate on mixing religion and politics. It answered some questions, but not others. The campaign produced a clear rejection of anti-Semitism; it showed that Americans reject efforts to claim a partisan monopoly on religion or virtue; it showed that they do not want clerics—whether John O'Connor or Jerry Falwell—telling them how to vote. The 1984 elections did not, however, provide any positive guidelines for "mixing religion and politics."

4. The Second Reagan Administration

"Watch What We Do, Not What We Say"

The 1984 election provided ample evidence of the ways in which religion and politics intermingle in America. But they don't mix only during election campaigns; they also mix during the life of an administration, in between elections. The first half of Ronald Reagan's second term in office provides dramatic examples of the many ways in which religion can be used improperly in political life.

THE PRESIDENT

Ronald Reagan successfully defused the religion-and-politics issue in 1984 by pledging to uphold the "wall of separation" between church and state. But the election was no sooner over than his administration began saying and doing things that made it clear that Reagan was in fact the president of the Dallas prayer breakfast, not of the B'nai B'rith speech. The second-term abuses of his administration were almost infinite in their variety, and leading the way was the president himself. After introducing his new budget, Reagan argued that "the Scriptures are on our side" in the battle to further increase US military spending. He cited Luke 14:31–32, in which Jesus tells of a king who had ten thousand men who had to make peace with another who had twenty thousand men. "I don't think we want to ever be in the position of being only half as strong and having to send a delegation to negotiate, under those circumstances, peace terms with the Soviet Union."

Even Reagan supporters like the Rev. Richard John Neuhaus of the Institute on Religion and Democracy and the Rev. Robert Dugan of the National Association of Evangelicals disagreed with the president's use of Scripture in this case. It was bad biblical scholarship to draw the conclusion Reagan did from the passage he cited; on the other hand, it was an improper use of religion to base a public policy directly on a biblical passage in any event; and, finally, Reagan was clearly trying to imply that those who disagreed with his budget priorities were unbiblical.

Having claimed that God was on his side on the military budget, it was not surprising that President Reagan claimed the support of a mere pope for his Central American policy. That claim prompted an unusual Vatican "clarification"—read "denial." The incident was the culmination of more than four years of administration misrepresentation of church positions and efforts to turn Catholic leaders against one another. It occurred in April 1985, when Reagan said he had received a message from the Pope John Paul "urging us to continue our efforts in Central America" and that the pope "has been most supportive of all of our efforts in Central America."

In a highly unusual development, Archbishop Pio Laghi, the Vatican Pro-nuncio, immediately denied that the pope could have supported "any concrete plan dealing, in particular, with military aspects." The next day the Vatican press office said that aside from the pope's comments to visiting US senators, which did not mention Central America, there had been no other messages from the pope. The statement noted that the Nicaraguan bishops had recently said that the pope's willingness to mediate between Nicaragua's Marxist government and the US-backed Contras "should not be interpreted as a political stand in favor of any party or ideology."

Reagan's claim about the pope was made at a conference on religious persecution cosponsored by the State Department, the National Association of Evangelicals, and the Institute for Religion and Democracy. The invitation to the conference promised that participants would include the president of the World Council of Churches and three Catholic cardinals—even though those people had not accepted invitations to speak. United Methodist Bishop LeRoy Hodapp of Indiana, member of the National Council of Churches' (NCC) governing board, says, "It was obvious to me that the primary issue of the conference was to lay it heavily on the NCC. The panel moderators turned even innocuous questions into heavy, heavy attacks."

(Administration officials developed a fondness for cosponsoring conferences with conservative religious groups. In August 1986, the Justice Department Office of Juvenile Justice and Delinquency Prevention sponsored a conference on the black family that was hosted in part by Pat Robertson.)

Despite the criticisms of his remarks about the Bible and the pope, Reagan continued to place himself on the side of the angels. When Congress scheduled a vote on aid to the Contras earlier than he had wanted, Reagan called the action "immoral," although most people would be hard pressed to see anything intrinsically moral or immoral in the scheduling of a vote. In the wake of controversy surrounding the revelation that a cemetery he planned to visit in Bitburg, West Germany, contained the graves of SS officers, Reagan rejected pressure to drop the visit. He told a group of foreign journalists, "I think it is morally right to do what I am doing, and I'm not going to change my mind about that." Yet it was precisely the morality of the Bitburg visit—and Reagan's related claim that German soldiers were as much victims of Hitler as those who died in concentration camps—that came under the sharpest attack.

But President Reagan was far from alone; religious excesses came from all parts of the administration. For example, the Office of Human Development Services within the Department of Health and Human Services sent sample sermons promoting adoption to five hundred child welfare agencies. "How blessed we are to have been chosen before the world was made to become adopted children through Jesus Christ," one of the sermons said. "... Let us open our minds and our hearts to our Christian and community responsibility and restore these children to their rightful place within the family."

Few people disagreed with the goal of encouraging adoption; but there was no need for the government to draft sermons for "Christians" or to tell people what their "Christian responsibility" was.

One bizarre incident involved two Cabinet agencies and the White House before it was played out. It began when Thomas Tancredo,

Denver regional representative for US Department of Education (DOE), used department stationary for a cover letter distributing copies of a speech by DOE's regional liaison, Robert Billings, former executive director of the Moral Majority, that described America as a "Christian nation." The letter, addressed to Christian school leaders in six states, referred with nostalgia to the days when "a number of states actually had state religions." It said that "godlessness is now controlling every aspect of our society" and that religion has been replaced by "secular humanism." The DOE later apologized to the American Jewish Congress for the mailing. Despite the fact that Reagan had disavowed the "Christian nation" movement during the campaign, Undersecretary of Education Gary Bauer said after a brief investigation that he saw nothing wrong with Tancredo's mailing.

But the story did not end there. Gerald Leib, a California attorney (and, coincidentally, a member of People for the American Way), wrote Tancredo protesting his "Christian nation" letter. Leib received an answer—from Christopher Sundseth, an aide at the Treasury Department. Sundseth told Leib, "We are, indeed, like it or not, a 'Christian nation' as more than 85 percent of adult Americans consider themselves 'Christians.' This country was founded by Christians who were escaping the same kind of small-minded tripe you espouse. The framers of the Constitution attempted specifically to anticipate those of your ilk who would try and abridge the very rights of freedom to worship guaranteed us by that document."

"You are a truly amazing, but pathetic creature," Sundseth continued. " . . . When you die, you will be giving account to Jesus Christ, your creator who happens himself to be a Christian. I hope you are prepared."

Sundseth said he obtained Leib's letter through unnamed "Christian activists" who used the Freedom of Information Act to obtain correspondence with federal agencies dealing with Christian issues; he said he often wrote letters to people whose names and letters he obtained this way. Sundseth's mother, Carolyn, was the White House religious liaison who had herself been in the headlines for her claim that aides around the president should "get saved or get out." Mrs. Sundseth told the Education Department Inspector General's Office of Investigation that she did not know how her son got Leib's letter; she described Leib as a "Norman Lear type" involved in a "pro-Jewish campaign being waged by Mr. Lear." Christopher Sundseth later lost his job as the result of budget cuts, and Mrs. Sundseth later left the White House to work for Pat Robertson's presidential campaign.

EDUCATION

While incidents of the improper mixing of religion and politics were likely to come from anywhere in the second Reagan term, they were most likely to come from two places—the Department of Education and the Department of Justice. President Reagan had made it clear that he would not endanger his popularity by pushing politically risky Religious Right positions, but he tolerated a great deal of unusual activity among his aides; because education and justice were the areas of greatest concern to the Religious Right, he made the greatest concessions in these areas. He allowed some thirty New Right and Religious Right groups to screen possible successors to Terrel Bell as Secretary of Education; William Bennett, then chairman of the National Endowment for the Humanities, went through the screening process, was approved, nominated, and confirmed by the Senate.

Before Bennett's tenure began, however, the Department issued two sets of regulations which fit neatly into the Religious Right's plans. Both involved legislation originally introduced by Senator Orrin Hatch (R-Utah). When the Senate debated a bill to restore funding for magnet schools, the Education for Economic Security Act, in 1984, Hatch attached an amendment barring the use of federal funds for programs teaching "secular humanism." The bill did not define the term, and the Department of Education issued regulations requiring local school districts to define "secular humanism." The regulations' impact was to give the Religious Right one more weapon with which to harass educators throughout the country. (The Senate, with Hatch's concurrence, dropped the "secular humanism" ban in October, 1985, after a campaign led by People for the American Way).

The second set of regulations applied to a Hatch Amendment attached to general education provisions in 1978. The amendment itself was not controversial; it required local school districts to allow parents to inspect any materials associated with experimental federal programs and required parental consent before students could be treated or tested psychologically or psychiatrically.

But the regulations expanded the number of programs covered by the amendment and broadened the definition of psychological and psychiatric examination, testing, and treatment to include virtually any school activity designed to elicit information about attitudes, habits, traits, opinions, beliefs, or feelings or designed to change behavior, attitudes, or emotions. The regulations were issued after hearings dominated by right-wing activists connected with Phyllis Schlafly's Eagle Forum. Schlafly's followers used the regulations to pressure local school districts on a wide variety of areas: in Hillsboro, Missouri, they attacked mock elections and state-mandated sex education programs; in Lincoln County, Oregon, they removed the entire student guidance and counseling program; in West Alexander, Florida, they attacked discussion of death and dying and the promotion of critical thinking in the elementary schools; and they objected to a number of drug and alcohol abuse programs.

One of the first controversies to engulf Bennett concerned his nomination of Eileen Marie Gardner, a Heritage Foundation analyst, as his special assistant for educational philosophy. Gardner drew fire for her comments on the handicapped and federal legislation guaranteeing them civil rights, but the reasoning—the theology—behind her comments raised larger issues. She had written for the Heritage Foundation that "the handicapped constituency displays a strange lack of concern for the effects of their regulations upon the welfare of the general population."

The handicapped, she wrote,

falsely assume that the lottery of life has penalized them at random. This is not so. Nothing comes to an individual that he has not, at some point in his development, summoned. When one blames his problems on external sources and thereby separates himself from a situation he has created, he is prevented from taking hold of and changing that part of himself which causes his difficulty. He becomes an ineffective malcontent who cannot evolve because he is separated from his source of change.

There is no injustice in the universe. As unfair as it may seem, a person's external circumstances *do* fit his level of inner spiritual development. The purpose (and the challenge) of life is for a person to take what he has and to use it for spiritual growth. Those of the handicapped constituency who seek to have others bear their burdens and eliminate their challenges are seeking to avoid the central issues of their lives.

The statements were sweeping in their hubris. At first, Bennett defended Gardner's right to her religious beliefs, which he called "Christian existentialism," but after a day of reaction, Bennett dropped the nomination like a hot potato. While Gardner was clearly entitled to her religious beliefs, she had no right to expect to bend the nation's policies toward the handicapped to fit them. But the issue was larger than the handicapped and larger than Eileen Gardner; James Dunn, executive director of the Baptist Joint Committee for Public Affairs, noted that "there is a hyper-Calvinism alive and well in the world that says 'If it is, it ought to be.' "

Bennett himself became the center of a new debate as he focused on the role of values and religion in education. The centerpiece was his August 7, 1985, speech to the Knights of Columbus. Bennett repeated Reagan's claim that "the Western ideas of freedom and democracy spring directly from the Judeo-Christian religious experience." Bennett attacked

four decades of misguided [Supreme] Court decisions [which] have thrust religion, and things touched by religion, out of the public schools.

Neutrality to religion turned out to bring with it a neutrality to those values that issue from religion. "Values clarification" flourished in our schools; but when public schools in Kentucky posted the Ten Commandments in classrooms, the Court found this unconstitutional. The Commandments were tainted, according to the Court, because they are "undeniably a sacred text in the Jewish and Christian faiths." And public school students cannot be exposed to any statement of such faiths. This, we are told, would violate the clear principle of separation of church and state, of religion and the public.

Our values as a free people and the central values of the Judeo-Christian tradition are flesh of the flesh, blood of the blood .... We now face a new source of divisiveness; the assault of secularism on religion. . . . We should not deny what is true: that from the Judeo-Christian tradition come our values, our principles, the animating spirit of our institutions. That tradition and our tradition are entangled. They are wedded together. When we have disdain for our religious tradition, we have disdain for ourselves.

Some of Bennett's concerns obviously had merit; there is a growing consensus that public schools do an inadequate job of teaching basic and civic values or teaching about the role of religion in history and culture. But Bennett spoke as though there were no sources for American values outside the Judeo-Christian tradition. He also misrepresented many of the Supreme Court's church-state decisions. The Kentucky Ten Commandments case, for example, did not say that students could not be exposed to the Commandments in the proper academic setting; it merely said they could not be displayed with the implication of state endorsement of sectarian values. Bennett said in the Knights of Columbus speech that he wanted to open "a national conversation and debate on the place of religious belief in our society." He was successful in doing that and later nuanced his own arguments much more carefully; his opening salvo, however, was simplistic and part of the Reagan administration effort to portray those who disagreed with its policies as antireligious.

JUSTICE

Bennett's counterpart at the Justice Department, Edwin Meese, had served as the New Right's leading champion in the White House before his controversial appointment as Attorney General. One of his controversial appointment as Attorney General. One of his first projects at Justice was an effort to reward an old friend and pay off the Religious Right. He planned to appoint Herbert Ellingwood, chairman of the federal Merit Systems Protection Board, as assistant attorney general in charge of legal policy, a post which oversees judicial appointments.

Ellingwood had already become the subject of controversy because of his involvement with the American Coalition for Traditional Values (ACTV) and its "Christian Talent Bank." ACTV leaders told the

Federal Times that Ellingwood was helping it achieve its goal of placing a quota of born-again Christians in political and civil service jobs. ACTV executive director Curtis Maynard said that when Ellingwood learns of civil service openings, "he submits them to us"; ACTV chairman Tim LaHaye had earlier said the organization wanted to "flood the bureaucracy with Christians." Ellingwood said he had suggested that ACTV recruit Christians for political appointments, but he denied advising the group on civil service openings.

Representative Patricia Schroeder (D-Colorado), chairman of the House civil service subcommittee, investigated Ellingwood's relationship with ACTV; while the subcommittee took no official action, Schroeder accused Ellingwood of showing "a total disregard for the whole idea of the merit system. He seems to think Christians have a corner on decency." In one speech to a Religious Right group, Ellingwood said, "For a person who doesn't know Jesus Christ, then religion is one thing and law is another, and our purpose is to show the proper interface of that." People for the American Way launched an unusual campaign to head off Ellingwood's nomination before it was made, and Meese decided against asking Reagan to nominate Ellingwood.

At the same time that he was trying to nominate Ellingwood, Meese was moving on the rhetorical front. He addressed the Knights of Columbus the same day as Bennett and echoed some of the same themes, citing Richard Neuhaus's image of the "naked public square": "Some people would interpret the First Amendment in a way that 'is extremely hurtful to the cause of religion,' " Meese said.

In its application, the principle of neutrality toward all religions has been transformed by some into hostility toward anything religious. . . . The application of strict neutrality to the public sphere has had the practical effect of forcing the exercise of religious faith into smaller and smaller private spheres. The danger is that religion could lose its social and historical—indeed, its public character. There are nations, we should remind ourselves, where religion has just this status.

Meese's most controversial speech on public religion, however, was his July 9, 1985, address to the American Bar Association (ABA) in which he called for a "Jurisprudence of Original Intention" and launched a major attack on the legal doctrine of incorporation, which holds that the Bill of Rights applies to the states as well as to the national government. The Supreme Court ruled in 1925 that the Fourteenth Amendment guarantee of equal protection had the effect of applying the Bill of Rights to the states. If the Bill of Rights did not apply to the states, the states would be able to ignore it; they could even establish their own official state religions. It's worth quoting from Meese's speech at length to give the full flavor of it—particularly in the light of a later backing off by the Justice Department:

In trying to make sense of the [Supreme Court] religion cases—from whatever side—it is important to remember how this body of tangled caselaw came about. Most Americans forget that it was not until 1925, in *Gitlow* v. *New York*, that *any* provision of the Bill of Rights was applied to the states. Nor was it until *1947* that the Establishment Clause was made applicable to the states through the 14th Amendment. This is striking because the Bill of Rights, as debated, created and ratified was designed to apply *only* to the national government.

The Bill of Rights came about largely as the result of the demands of the critics of the new Constitution, the unfortunately misnamed Anti-Federalists. They feared, as George Mason of Virginia put it, that in time the national authority would "devour" the states. Since each state had a Bill of Rights, it was only appropriate that so powerful a national government as that created by the Constitution have one as well. Though Hamilton insisted a Bill of Rights was not necessary and even destructive, and Madison (at least at first) thought a Bill of Rights to be but a "parchment barrier" to political power, the Federalists agreed to add a Bill of Rights.

Though the first ten amendments that were ultimately ratified fell far short of what the Anti-Federalists desired, both Federalists and Anti-Federalists agreed that the amendments were a curb on national power.

When this view was questioned before the Supreme Court in *Barron* v. *Baltimore* (1833), Chief Justice Marshall wholeheartedly agreed. The Constitution said what it meant and meant what it said. Neither political expediency nor judicial desire was sufficient to change the clear import of the language of the Constitution. The Bill of Rights did not apply to the states—and, he said, that was that.

Until 1925, that is.

Since then a good portion of constitutional adjudication has been aimed at extending the scope of the doctrine of incorporation. But the most that can be done is to expand the scope; nothing can be done to shore up the intellectually shaky foundation upon which the foundation rests. And nowhere else has the principle of federalism been dealt so politically violent and constitutionally suspect a blow as by the theory of incorporation.

Within the context of this discussion, Meese said "to have argued, as is popular today, that the [First] amendment demands a strict neutrality between religion and irreligion would have struck the founding generation as bizarre. The purpose was to prohibit religious tyranny, not to undermine religion generally."

Meese's speech was widely criticized, and two sitting Supreme Court justices took the highly unusual step of responding directly to his arguments. In an October 12, 1985, speech at Georgetown University, Justice William Brennan said,

There are those who find legitimacy in fidelity to what they call "the intentions of the Framers." In its most doctrinaire incarnation, this view demands that Justices discern exactly what the Framers thought about the question under consideration and simply follow that intention in resolving the case before them.

It is a view that feigns self-effacing deference to the specific judgment of those who forged our original social compact. But in truth it is little more than arrogance cloaked as humility. It is arrogant to pretend that from our vantage we can gauge accurately the intent of the Framers on application of principle to specific, contemporary questions. All too often, sources of potential enlightenment such as records of the ratification debates provide sparse or ambiguous evidence of the original intention.

Typically, all that can be gleaned is that the Framers themselves did not agree about the application or meaning of particular constitutional provisions, and hid their differences in cloaks of generality. Indeed, it is far from clear whose intention is relevant—that of the drafters, the congressional disputants, or the ratifiers in the states?—or even whether the idea of an original intention is a coherent way of thinking about a jointly drafted document drawing its authority from a general assent of the states. And apart from the problematic nature of the sources, our distance of two centuries cannot but work as a prism refracting all we perceive.

As one of the court's leading liberals, Brennan might have been expected to reject Meese's views. But on October 23, one of the court's moderates, Justice John Paul Stevens, also weighed in against

Meese. Unlike Brennan, however, Stevens took him on by name and responded to direct quotes in his ABA speech. He focused on Meese's attack on the doctrine of incorporation:

Of course the Attorney General has correctly stated the holding in *Barron* v. *Baltimore* in 1833, and he was quite correct in identifying the year 1925 as the time when the Supreme Court first held that the State of New York, as well as the Congress of the United States, must obey the dictates of the First Amendment. The development of his argument is somewhat incomplete, however, because its concentration on the original intention of the Framers of the Bill of Rights overlooks the importance of subsequent events in the development of our law. In particular, it overlooks the profound importance of the Civil War and the post-war Amendments on the structure of our government, and particularly upon the relationship between the Federal Government and the separate states. Moreover, the Attorney General fails to mention the fact that no Justice who has sat on the Court during the past sixty years has questioned the proposition that the prohibitions against state action that are incorporated in the Fourteenth Amendment include the prohibitions against federal action that are found in the First Amendment.

Stevens also questioned Meese's use of the term "founding generation," which, he said, "describes a rather broad and diverse class. It included apostles of intolerance as well as tolerance, advocates of differing points of view in religion as well as politics, and great minds in Virginia and Pennsylvania as well as Massachusetts. I am not at all sure that men like James Madison, Thomas Jefferson, Benjamin Franklin, or the pamphleteer, Thomas Paine, would have regarded strict neutrality on the part of government between religion and irreligion as 'bizarre.' "

On November 9, 1985, a letter from Terry Eastland, director of the Justice Department Office of Public Affairs, appeared in *The Washington Post* reintrepreting Meese's ABA speech. "Meese did not say in his July American Bar Association address that 'the Bill of Rights should not be applied to the States' . . . Meese has never said that." Eastland's clarification was reassuring; but no one who heard or read the speech could be blamed for believing that Meese, in fact, believed that the Bill of Rights should not apply to the states.

If Meese backed off somewhat from his own rhetoric, however, he did not back off from his plan to fill the federal judiciary with people who could pass the New Right's ideological litmus tests. The appointment of judges is, by its very nature, a political action. There is no doubt that Democrats tend to appoint mostly Democrats, Republicans appoint Republicans, liberals appoint liberals, and conservatives appoint conservatives. All of this normally happens, however, within a context of appointing qualified people who, whatever their philosophic views, respect the legal system. The requirement of Senate confirmation for judicial appointments is a necessary check on the power of the president to shape the federal judiciary.

The ideological prescreening of judicial nominees first surfaced when Senators John East, Jeremiah Denton, and Orrin Hatch asked Josph Rodriguez, a nominee from New Jersey, to answer a questionnaire asking his positions on abortion, affirmative action, vouchers, school prayer, the death penalty, the constitutionality of the National Labor Relations Act, and whether it makes a difference in arguing a case that "moral beliefs are based on a belief in the existence of a Supreme Being." The questionnaire also asked Rodriguez to list all political contributions of more than $15 for the past ten years.

Rodriguez was Public Advocate of New Jersey, a member of Republican governor Tom Kean's cabinet and former head of the state Bar Association. He was exceptionally well qualified for a district judgeship, he had strong political support, and East, Denton, and Hatch angered Judiciary Committee Chairman Strom Thurmond by going behind his back with their questionnaire. Rodriguez was confirmed, but the issue of ideological prescreening was now public, and the administration's own ideological prescreening became an issue. The best way to understand the strength of such prescreening in the Reagan Justice Department is to compare the backgrounds of those viewed as not sufficiently pure ideologically and those for whom the administration made an all-out fight. These candidates for federal judgeships were rejected:

- Judith Whittaker, a Republican, associate general counsel of Hallmark cards, first in her law school class, rated highly by the ABA, and described as "outstanding" by the Chief Justice of the US Court of Appeals for the 8th District. The White House removed her from consideration for an appointment after right-wing groups charged that she had supported the Equal Rights Amendment and was proabortion, even though she had never stated her views on abortion publicly.

- Andrew Frey, deputy solicitor-general of the United States and the government's chief advocate on criminal issues before the Supreme Court. He was proposed for a seat on the Washington, D.C., Court of Appeals, but his name was withdrawn after it was revealed that he had made small contributions to Planned Parenthood and the National Coalition to Ban Handguns.

- William Hellerstein, appeals chief of the New York City Legal Aid Society, was recommended for a district court post by New York Senators Daniel Patrick Moynihan, a Democrat, and Alfonse D'Amato, a Republican; he was endorsed by twenty-four former federal prosecutors and by prominent Republicans, including President Ford's former deputy attorney general, Harold Tyler. The administration backed off the appointment after Roy Cohn, former aide to Senator Joe McCarthy, denounced him as an "ultraliberal" because fifteen years earlier he had written an article critical of imprisoning people for minor drug-possession crimes, prostitution, and gambling.

These are some of the judges whose nominations were high priorities for the Reagan administration:

- Sid Fitzwater, who had been involved in a 1982 Republican "ballot security" operation which posted intimidating signs in minority neighborhoods in Dallas warning of penalties for vote fraud. The Reagan Justice Department civil rights division was critical of the action, but the administration stood behind Fitzwater's appointment to the US District court in Dallas. He was confirmed, after supporters broke a filibuster, by a 52 to 42 vote; at the time, this was the closest vote so far on a Reagan judicial nominee.

- Jeffrey Sessions of Alabama. He had called the National Association for The Advancement of Colored People (NAACP) and the American Civil Liberties Union (ACLU) "un-American" and "Communist-inspired" organizations "trying to force civil rights down the throats of people"; he once described a white civil rights lawyer as a "disgrace to his race" and said he thought the Ku Klux Klan was "OK, until I learned they smoke pot." Sessions's nominated was defeated in the Senate Judiciary Committee.

- Lino Graglia, a Texas law professor. Graglia told a Texas community it was "under no obligation" to obey federal court busing orders; he admitted calling black children "pickaninnies"; and was found unqualified by the ABA. Despite the negative ABA rating, the administration looked for justification to nominate him and asked Griffin Bell, Attorney General under Jimmy Carter, to examine Graglia's record and to recommend whether he should be nominated for a federal judgeship; Bell recommended against a nomination.

- Daniel Manion, a forty-four-year-old former Indiana state legislator working in private practice at the time of his nomination to the prestigious Court of Appeals for the Seventh Circuit, covering Illinois, Indiana, and Wisconsin. Manion became the most controversial of the Reagan court appointees. He had little substantive legal experience and had never written a scholarly law article. Research by People for the American Way's Ricki Seidman showed that he shared many of the views of his father, Clarence Manion, a founder of the John Birch Society. The younger Manion had opposed the application of the Bill of Rights to the states; he had praised the John Birch Society for being "on the front line of the fight for constitutional freedom"; while in the legislature, he had sponsored a bill to authorize posting the Ten Commandments on public school walls only a few months after the Supreme Court had overturned a similar law in Kentucky. Manion faced stiff opposition; Senator Edward Kennedy (D-Massachusetts) called him "the least qualified appellate nominee submitted to the United States Senate by any president of either party since I have been in the Senate."

On June 26, 1986, the Senate confirmed Manion by 48 to 46 after Senator Slade Gorton (R-Washington), who at first opposed Manion, changed his vote after being promised by the White House that it would move on his nominee for a federal judicial post. In a parliamentary maneuver, the Democrats obtained a reconsideration of the vote; but on July 23, 1986, the Senate confirmed Manion by 50 to 49, with Vice President Bush casting the deciding vote.

A Peter Hart Poll conducted for People for the American Way in July 1986 showed that the Reagan administration's court-packing strategy was at odds with public opinion:

- 78 percent of Americans agreed that "It is important for the Senate to make sure that the judges on the Supreme Court represent a balanced point of view"; only 16 percent agreed that "The Senate should let a president put whomever he wants on the Supreme Court, so long as the person is honest and competent."

- 77 percent said it was a "bad idea for a president to consider only people who believe government should be able to restrict a woman's right to choice on abortion" in making appointments to the federal courts; only 14 percent said it was a "good idea." In fact, even those who believed that the Supreme Court's abortion decisions should be reversed agreed by 59 to 31 percent that it would be wrong to make this position a prerequisite for a court appointment; 57 percent of those surveyed said a person's commitment to repealing the court's abortion decisions was a valid reason for opposing his or her confirmation, while 38 percent said it was not a valid reason.

- 96 percent said "state and local governments should be required to abide by the Bill of Rights"; only 2 percent disagreed.

- 76 percent agreed that "In making decisions, the Supreme Court should consider changing times and modern realities in applying the principles of the Constitution"; 17 percent disagreed.

- 57 percent disagreed with the statement, "In making decisions, the Supreme Court should only consider the original intent of the Founding Fathers when they wrote the Constitution two hundred years ago"; 34 percent agreed.

- While 52 percent said the court decisions banning organized group prayer in the schools should be reversed, Americans, by 71 percent to 17 percent, supported "the decisions that require the government to maintain a strict separation of church and state."

- Table 1 shows on a scale of 1 to 10, with 10 the most important, the way Americans, in the Hart/People for the American Way poll, rated their considerations about nominees to the Supreme Court and other federal courts.

CONCLUSION

In the second Reagan administration, President Reagan and key officials, particularly William Bennet and Edwin Meese, consistently drew a line: on one side, they placed themselves, God, the Bible, and the Judeo-Christian tradition; on the other side, they placed all those who disagreed with them on school prayer, abortion, the independent judiciary, or other issues. The administration tolerated militant Fundamentalists—such as Ellingwood, Tancredo, and the Sundseth family—who treated those who had not been "born again" as second-class citizens. It mounted an assault on the separation of powers and the Bill of Rights, giving legitimacy and support to the most radical elements within the Religious Right.

All this happened after Reagan pledged before B'nai B'rith to uphold the "wall of separation" between church and state. The second Reagan administration recalled the words of Richard Nixon's attorney general, John Mitchell: "Don't watch what we say, watch what we do."

But the Reagan administration record is important beyond the personality of Ronald Reagan; it provides detailed evidence of what can happen in any administration solicitous of its ties to the Religious Right.

5. The 1986 Midterm Elections

"God Told Me to Run"

Midterm elections have a different dynamic than presidential elections; they tend to be more local and diffuse in focus without the dominating issue of a presidential race. The 1986 elections were no exception; it was not until after the election that analysts could point to concern about the state of the economy as the major campaign issue. But another issue ranked close behind—the mixing of religion and politics. The 1986 elections saw growing evidence of religious intolerance, continued evidence of the many ways in which religion and politics are entwined; they also saw important shifts within the Religious Right.

RELIGIOUS INTOLERANCE AND PARTISAN RELIGION

The 1986 elections saw several significant examples of both the partisan use of religion and outright religious intolerance in addition to the activities of the Religious Right, which we will examine in detail shortly.

- In the primary to determine the Republican nominee for a vacant seat in Texas's 21st Congressional District, Van Archer said he "would think" that his opponent's religion would be an issue; he said that if Lamar Smith, a Christian Scientist, were elected to Congress and legislation involving health treatment arose, he would have to choose between being a good congressman and a good Christian Scientist. Christian Scientists believe that prayer and understanding will cure sickness and avoid medical treatment for themselves, but do not impose their views on others.

  Smith said he had not faced such a conflict as a state representative or as a county commissioner. He said, "I believe in the best medical attention for those who want it"—and, in fact, he was endorsed by the American Medical Association. Smith said, "Attacking an individual's religion is an attack on one of our most sacred institutions—freedom of religion. It has no place in American society." Smith won the nomination.

- In Maryland, Republican Linda Chavez was both the target of religious bigotry and the practitioner of religious partisanship. The first issue concerned reports that Chavez, who was raised a Catholic and still calls herself a Catholic, had converted to Judaism when she married her husband. In a primary debate, another candidate, Michael Schaefer, told Chavez, "I don't know if you're Catholic or Jewish. You have a Catholic background and a Jewish family."

But Chavez herself attempted to use religious affiliation in a partisan way in the general election against Representative Barbara Mikulski. Chavez charged that Mikulski was behind stories about her conversion; Mikulski denied the charge. Chavez later wrote a letter to Catholics in the state saying, "The very last thing I want to do is to write you a letter appealing to you as a Catholic, but religious intolerance and bigotry have left me no choice." At the same time Chavez was distributing this letter, Senator Rudy Boschwitz (R-Minnesota), who is Jewish, sent a letter to Jews in Maryland saying Chavez's relationship to the Jewish community was unique because of her support for Israel, her opposition to quotas, and her marriage to Christopher Gersten, a Jewish activist. Chavez lost in a landslide—with 88 percent of Maryland's Jews and 66 percent of its Catholics voting for Mikulski.

- Republican leaders also made another direct appeal to religious affiliation in the Missouri Senate race between Kit Bond and Democrat Harriet Woods. In a letter sanctioned by Boschwitz, President Reagan and Senate Majority Leader Bob Dole, four Republican fund-raisers—Max Fisher, Richard Fox, George Klein, and Ivan Boesky (who was later convicted of insider stock trading on Wall Street)—criticized Woods, who is Jewish, on the grounds that "her children were raised as Protestants." Bond won, but the fund-raising letter was not an issue because it came to light only after the election.

- In Pennsylvania, Democrat Bob Casey, the successful gubernatorial candidate, sent out a last-minute mailgram implying that the past religious affiliation of his opponent, Republican Bill Scranton, was not a good role model for children: "Then he grew bored with journalism and became a disciple of Marharishi Mahesh Yogi, traveling the world evangelizing for Transcendental Meditation."

LYNDON LAROUCHE

Religious bigotry was also an issue in the effort of followers of Lyndon LaRouche to win state and congressional seats in the 1986 elections. The major upset of the political season occurred in Illinois on March 16 when two LaRouche followers defeated regular party candidates for the Democratic nominations for Lieutenant Governor (Mark Fairchild) and Secretary of State (Janice Hart). Two other LaRouche candidates won primaries for congressional seats in heavily Republican districts—Domenick Jeffrey in the Thirteenth District and William J. Brenner, Sr., in the Fifteenth District.

LaRouche and his followers called themselves the National Democratic Policy Committee to create the false impression that they were associated with the official Democratic Party. They claimed to have fielded candidates in 7 Senate races, 146 congressional races, and 7 governor's races, and a total of 780 candidates nationwide in 29 states.

LaRouche is a former Leninist who has moved to the extreme right. Conservatives say he is really a leftist, and liberals say he is really a right-winger, but LaRouche operates in a twilight zone where the extreme left and extreme right meet. He is best-known for his bizarre conspiracy theories in which the Queen of England is a drug dealer and Henry Kissinger and Walter Mondale are Soviet Agents.

But a key part of LaRouche's agenda consists of classic religious bigotry. He has had friendly contacts with both the racist and anti-Semitic Liberty Lobby and the Ku Klux Klan; his tone became more anti-Semitic after making those contacts around 1974. LaRouche once sued the Anti-Defamation League (ADL) for libel because it called him anti-Semitic; in October 1980, a New York State Supreme Court justice dismissed the suit and said calling LaRouche anti-Semitic was "fair comment" and that the facts in the case "reasonably give rise" to the ADL characterization.

LaRouche believes that there is an international Jewish conspiracy to control the world; that it involves Jewish bankers and the drug lobby; that prominent Jews installed Hitler; that the Holocaust was a Jewish hoax because the Nazis killed "only . . . about a million-and-a-half" Jews. He has called the ADL "a treasonous conspiracy" against the United States and said it "today resurrects the tradition of the Jews who demanded the crucifixion of Christ." LaRouche has said that there is "a hard kernel of truth" in the Protocols of the Elders of Zion, an anti-Semitic forgery first published in the nineteenth century and purporting to reveal a Jewish plot for world domination.

LaRouche believes that the Catholic church is controlled by the "Anglo-Jesuit penetration" using Georgetown University as a base as part of the international Zionist conspiracy; that British intelligence controls the World Council of Churches, which in turn controls the National Council of Churches, which in turn control US Protestant church bodies. According to *Insight,* published by *The Washington Times,* LaRouche believes that the Women's Christian Temperance Union was "a violent cult of ax-wielding lesbians."

After the Illinois primaries, the Democratic National Committee publicized and attacked LaRouche candidates and defeated them in all of eighty-five contested races. Six LaRouche candidates won uncontested races, but all were easily defeated in the general election.

LaRouche backers had a major nonelectoral victory in California. They gathered enough signatures to place an initiative on the California ballot in November that would redefine AIDS as an infectious disease—like measles or tuberculosis—and pressure public health officials to quarantine AIDS victims and those suspected of carrying the virus. Medical officials and politicians across the state organized a group called Stop LaRouche to fight the initiative, which opponents said had no justifiable public health purpose. LaRouche backers gathered 683,576 signatures, nearly twice the number necessary to qualify the initiative for the ballot; but many of the signatures were collected by LaRouche workers carrying signs that said only "Sign here to help stop AIDS."

A bipartisan coalition of political, civic, and religious leaders including both party's candidates for governor, the state council of churches, and the state's Catholic bishops campaigned against the AIDS initiative. The initiative lost by a 2-to-1 margin.

THE RELIGIOUS RIGHT

Religious Right political activity in 1986 changed in two significant ways from previous years. First, it concentrated heavily on grassroots organizing and recruiting candidates at the local level. In 1985, Jerry Falwell and Tim LaHaye had said more Fundamentalists would run for office at the local level, and that is exactly what happened. This grassroots emphasis was sparked by the encouragement of national leaders as well as the spontaneous effort of local people encouraged by the Religious Right's past success. LaHaye told an October 1985 meeting of the American Coalition for Traditional Values (ACTV), "If every Bible-believing church in America would trust God to use them to raise up one person to run for public office in the next ten years, do you realize that we would have more Christians in office than there are offices to hold?" He said an ACTV plan to increase grassroots activity to keep the Republicans from losing the Senate was "a workable plan, and it's a plan that God wants us to fulfill." Pat Robertson in particular, through the Freedom Council, used veteran political activists to organize Fundamentalists at the local level. The grassroots emphasis included Christian Voice's inclusion of candidates for governor, lieutenant governor, and state legislature in its *Biblical Scoreboard* activity within the Republican Party.

The second major shift for the Religious Right in 1986 was giving up any pretense of being nonpartisan; the movement launched efforts to take over the Republican party in Indiana, Iowa, Maryland,

Michigan, Minnesota, Nebraska, North Carolina, Oregon, South Carolina, and Texas; it had a significant influence on party platforms in Iowa, Missouri, Nebraska, Texas, and several other states.

The Republicans continued to court the Religious Right while the movement was busy at work trying to overthrow the party establishment. During the final weeks of the campaign, the Republican Senatorial Campaign Committee ran a radio ad in Alabama, North Carolina, and Florida which said, "Ever think what's important to you? It's probably simple—a steady job, a healthy family, and a personal relationship with Christ." The ad was discontinued after protests from Jewish organizations and People for the American Way.

The Republican Congressional Campaign Committee paid for a letter sent out by Jackie McGregor, the Republican candidate in the 3rd District in Michigan, in which McGregor attacked Representative Howard Wolpe: "California actor Ed Asner and Howard Wolpe are raising money by sending a letter to one-half million members of their religion outside our district"; Wolpe and Asner are Jewish. In 1984, McGregor had used a letter from Representative Mark Siljander calling on voters to "send another Christian to Congress."

Vice President George Bush tried to have it both ways with the Religious Right. He had earlier sought and accepted Jerry Falwell's endorsement for the 1988 presidential race and had told a Falwell conference, "What great goals you have!" Campaigning in South Carolina, he said it was necessary to elect Republicans in order "to do the Lord's work at the state level." But when Robertson forces made a strong run at Bush in the Michigan caucuses, Bush supporters distributed a flyer saying "Keep Religion out of Politics."

(The Republicans were not the only party to indulge in religious bigotry. Democratic National Committee Chairman Paul Kirk sent out a fund-raising letter in December 1985, which, in attacking Pat Robertson, equated all Evangelical Christians with the Religious Right. It criticized Robertson not simply for supporting a quota system for Fundamentalists in government, but for wanting to "get more Christians involved in government." Kirk said in a postscript, "When President Pat Robertson finishes his Scripture reading and begins his televised State of the Union address, it will be too late"—

implying that a president does not have the right to read the Bible.)

Religious Right grassroots activity in 1986 took a variety of forms:

Alaska

State Senator Edna DeVries, a candidate for the Republican nomination for lieutenant governor, said she was a candidate because God told her to run. She told *The Anchorage Times:* "Some would say, 'Edna, you have a safe seat, why are you doing this?' When God speaks, you need to be obedient. I want to look back on 1986 and be able to say, 'God, I have done what you asked me to do, gone where you told me to go, and said what you wanted me to say.' Her husband Noel said in a fund-raising letter, "Edna is running for Lt. Governor simply because she believes God is directing her to run."

According to *Church and State* magazine, she believes the United States is a Christian country and that those who disagree "have a right to do what they want, but they shouldn't live in the United States. Maybe they should live in some other country. If they don't honor the United States as a Christian nation and they don't want to be a Christian, then there are many other countries that are not Christian."

Arizona

Footprints, a Fundamentalist newspaper printed in the Phoenix area, published a "Christian Voting Guide for Primary Election Sept. 9" and promised a similar "Christian Voting Guide" for the general election. In *Footprints,* a Republican candidate in the 19th State Senate District ran an ad saying, "Elect Jan Brewer State Senator—Vote for a Christian." And Democrat J. "Sookie" Charles, running for state representative for the 22nd District, ran an ad which said, "Lord, we acknowledge that we have not sought you and your kingdom above all things. Create new hearts in us and give us the courage to risk what we have and who we are for your sake and the gospel's." Former Representative John Conlan, head of the FaithAmerica Foundation, ran unsuccessfully for the 4th District House seat he gave up in an unsuccessful run for the Senate in 1976; that year, he was accused of using anti-Semitism in his primary contest against Representative Sam Steiger, who is Jewish.

California

In the Twenty-Seventh District, Republican candidate Rob Scribner picked up where he left off in 1984 in his unsuccessful effort to unseat Representative Mel Levine. In a letter to pastors in his district, he said:

A year ago, God did a rather unique thing—he called me to run for Congress in California's 27th District. . . . When God requires a thing of you, you must obey. . . . Encourage your congregation to vote . . . teach them to vote based on the relationship of the issues and the Word of God. Teach them not to vote according to party or personality, but according to the candidates' integrity before God. . . . I am committed to the vision God is pointing me toward. . . . Mr. Levine . . . is diametrically opposed to nearly everything the Lord's church stands for in this nation. . . . I hope you will agree to link arms with us as we literally "take territory" for our Lord Jesus Christ.

Colorado

The Republican senatorial candidate, Representative Ken Kramer, was a member of Christian Voice's congressional advisory board. Pat Robertson endorsed Kramer in the primary for the Senate seat being vacated by Gary Hart. Ted Strickland, Republican candidate for governor, called for a "Christian-centered" government during an interview on a Fundamentalist radio program the night before the primary election.

Florida

Bob Plimpton, Freedom Council coordinator for South Florida, distributed a flyer at Palm Beach County churches which said, "Wanted: Qualified Christian Candidates for Palm Beach County School Board. . . . If you are willing to pray about becoming a candidate, please call Bob Plimpton . . . fear not, we can train you and get you elected with God's help." (Three Religious Right candidates were overwhelmingly defeated).

In the Sixteenth Congressional District, Republican challenger Mary Collins distributed material saying, "His positions on infanticide, gun control, abortion, and prayer in the school make Larry Smith the antithesis of what the Christian community in the District would prefer."

Georgia

In the Seventh Congressional District, Democrat Buddy Darden was challenged by the Rev. Joe Morecraft, minister of the late Representative Larry McDonald, a John Bircher who held the seat until his death in 1983. Morecraft is a member of a splinter group of Presbyterian Fundamentalists called "theonomists," who believe that civil law must conform to biblical law.

Two fund-raisers who supported Representative Pat Swindall in his defeat of incumbent Elliott Levitas in 1984, James Zauderer and Nancy Schaefer, sent out a fund-raising letter for Morecraft in which they referred to Swindall and said, "God has provided another man who is willing to serve Our Lord in the Halls of Congress." In another fund-raising letter, David and Marlene Goodrum said, "Imagine what kind of nation the United States would be if the Senate, the House of Representatives, and the Supreme Court had the commitment to Christ and the knowledge and dedication to God's Word that Joe Morecraft has."

Idaho

In the governor's race, Republican Dave LeRoy used national party campaign funds to produce and distribute bookmarks that have his name on one side and Jesus' on the other.

Indiana

In the First Congressional District, State Senator William Costas "said that a message from God was the reason he entered the race in the heavily Democratic 1st District," according to the *Gary Post-Tribune*. The paper quoted Costas: "I said, Lord, you have to show me. I was waiting for bright lights and a voice out of the sky, but that didn't happen. So I said, Lord, show my wife. And one day, when she was driving home from Indianapolis, she had the thought that God was telling her that 'This thing with you husband is of me and you should encourage him to run.' That was the important step."

In the Third Congressional District, Donald Lynch, associate minister of the Beachgrove Nazarene Church, upset Jay Whitcliff, another establishment candidate. Lynch, who had help from Greg Dixon, head of the Indiana Moral Majority, based his campaign on a crusade against AIDS carriers, running an ad that asked "AIDS—Is there a Cover-up?" He pledged to support legislation which would, among other things, "cut off revenue sharing funds to cities which fail to close illicit public bathhouses."

In the Fifth District, State Senator James Butcher defeated State Treasurer James Ridlin, the candidate of party leaders. Butcher received help from Pat Robertson, who raised $30,000 for him at a fund-raiser.

Iowa

Fundamentalists organized by Steve Sheffler, a Freedom Council worker, dominated Republican Party caucuses in four counties, including the area of Des Moines. They tried to purge party regulars: Mary Louise Smith, former director of the Republican National Committee, was elected a delegate only after five ballots, when she convinced Fundamentalists that her experience would be valuable.

While party regulars retained control, they made major concessions to the Fundamentalists on the platform. Resolutions adopted June 21, 1986, included a call for the teaching of creationism in public schools. The platform also included this plank:

Whereas the words "separation of church and state" do not appear anywhere in the US Constitution,

Whereas the Supreme Court Justice William Rehnquist has termed the phrase a "misleading metaphor" that should be abandoned,

We sincerely desire that the First Amendment of the Constitution be interpreted and applied according to the intent of the Framers, which provided for religion rather than freedom from religion.

This phrase "separation of church and state" which appears in the Constitution of the Soviet Union has regularly been used to exclude Godly principles, and we believe this violates the heritage of this nation and the spirit upon which it was founded.

Maryland

Several Fundamentalist activists in Maryland were elected to Republican Central Committee posts. In Charles County, seven candidates with ties to the New Covenant Church in Waldorf ran as a slate for the Central Committee; three were elected. Ousted committee members, including the chairman, Marvin Green, claimed the Fundamentalists had used deception by distributing leaflets which created the impression that they were backed by the committee. Three other members of New Covenant Church ran for school board on a pro-creationism, pro-home schooling platform. In Silver Spring, at least fifteen members of two Fundamentalist churches—the Great Commission Church and Damascus Christian Community—ran for seats on the Republican Central Committee; another four from the two churches ran for the Democratic Central Committee. Four of the GOP candidates were elected; none of the Democratic candidates were elected, but regular party candidates claim the church candidates drew votes which cost them.

Nebraska

Rev. Everett Sileven sent out a fund-raising letter in his unsuccessful attempt to win the Republican gubernatorial nomination which said, "I have God. I know I can count on God. Can I count on you? . . . I thank you and God thanks you." When both parties nominated women for governor, Sileven said, "Biblically and constitutionally, it is a great step backward. Jeremiah plainly tells us that when the people of a nation are willing to accept the leadership of a woman, it is a sure sign of God's curse."

At the Douglas and Lincoln County Republican convention, which includes Omaha and Lincoln, the Religious Right made major gains in electing delegates to the state convention. Freedom Council state coordinator Bob Garrett successfully controlled delegate selection in Douglas county.

North Carolina

The Rev. Kent Kelly of Southern Pines, sent out a letter supporting James Broyhill, named to fill John East's Senate seat, and accusing Democratic Senate candidate Terry Sanford of favoring a "one-world government." Kelly said, "We know what government that is—that which is foretold in the Book of Revelation." (One of the tenets of Armageddon theology is that a one-world government is a sign of the coming of the Anti-christ).

Broyhill himself had to fight off a challenge from Jesse Helms's Congressional Club and its senatorial candidate, David Funderbunk, despite having a 100 percent rating from Citizens for Constitutional Action and a 75 percent rating from Christian Voice. Funderbunk and other Religious right activists said Broyhill was too liberal because he had once voted for the Equal Rights Amendment and had voted to make Martin Luther King's birthday a national holiday.

Funderbunk actively courted Fundamentalist groups. Among other efforts, he responded to a questionnaire prepared by a group called Students for Better Government which included these questions: "Can you honestly say that you have a personal relationship with Jesus Christ? How well do you know him?" and "If you answered yes ... would you, if elected, seek God's guidance for your decisions? If no, how would you determine your answers and solutions?" Funderbunk's answers included this: "I think that only by a strong belief in the Lord can we restore the foundation values of the value of human life, the family, home and church (and a fixed right and wrong) as central to our country's survival. ... I stand for conservative beliefs and traditional values to keep this nation free and one Blessed by God ... I believe in Jesus Christ as my Lord and Savior, relying on his guidance first."

In the Fourth District, Representative William Cobey, who won with Religious Right backing in 1984, distributed a fund-raising letter addressed "Dear Christian Friend," which said, "As an ambassador for Christ, I see my ministry to the other members of Congress as twofold: as an encourager, and as a Christian example. ... Will you help me so our voice will not be silenced and then replaced by someone who is not willing to take a strong stand for the principles outlined in the Word of God?"

Cobey's opponent, David Price, was a Southern Baptist graduate of Yale Divinity School who taught political science and ethics at

Duke University. Cobey had a 100 percent Christian Voice rating, Price a 17. Cobey lost, and his letter was considered a major factor.

Ohio

A letter sent out by the campaign of Republican gubernatorial candidate James Rhodes and addressed "Dear Christian Leader" declared, "As a leader under God's authority, you cannot afford to resign yourself to idle neutrality in an election that will determine the future moral environment of our state. . . . It is vital you know that there is a distinct contrast between Dick Celeste and Jim Rhodes on the question of traditional family values."

In a letter mailed on Rhodes's behalf, the Ohio Citizens for Decency and Health Political Action Committee (PAC) said, "The Lord is calling for mighty men of God who will stand in the gap for our land, that God should not destroy it."

Republican Senate candidate Tom Kindness accused Senator John Glenn of waging wars on Fundamentalist Christians; Glenn had attacked the Religious Right.

James Condit, Jr., an antiabortion leader in the Cincinnati area, said that groups like Planned Parenthood, the American Civil Liberties Union (ACLU), and the National Organization of Women (NOW) are part of "an anti-Christian network whose cause is to work for anti-Christian goals. That network is overly peopled by members of the Reform Jewish community and men who I believe to be Free Masons."

Oregon

Joe Lutz, a thirty-five-year-old Fundamentalist Baptist minister, won a surprising 43 percent of the vote against Senator Bob Packwood in the Republican primary. Lutz spent less than $50,000, while Packwood spent $2 million on TV ads and phone banks. Lutz received organizational and other help from the Freedom Council, the American Coalition for Traditional Values, and Concerned Women for America and claimed to have five thousand church-based volunteers.

Pennsylvania

Richard Stokes ran an unsuccessful campaign in the Republican primary against Senator Arlen Spector because, he said, God told him to run. He said, "We feel that we have checked and rechecked that and that we were doing what He wanted us to do."

South Carolina

The Religious Right mounted a strong challenge to Dr. George Graham, the South Carolina Republican party chairman, who was reelected only after promising to give the chairmanship to the Fundamentalists after this year's election.

South Dakota

Dale Bell, a Religious Right activist who has worked for the National Conservative Political Action Committee and the Conservative Caucus, won the Republican primary to run for the House seat that was vacated by Thomas Daschle, who ran for the Senate. Bell was endorsed by Pat Robertson and received funds from Robertson's Committee for Freedom PAC.

Tennessee

In the Third District, Pat Robertson endorsed Jim Golden in the Republican primary; Golden defeated John Davis, who had held Democrat Marilyn Lloyd to 52 percent of the vote in 1984. (The victory of Lloyd, a member of the Christian Voice Congressional Advisory Committee, in 1984 was viewed as a Religious Right victory.) Lloyd was reelected.

Texas

Religious Right activists tried to remove George Strake as state party chairman in Texas, but were unsuccessful. A related effort in the state came from the Texas Grassroots Coalition PAC, led by Adrian Van Zelfden, which asked candidates in the state Fifth and Tenth Districts to sign a "Believers' Decree of Agreement." (Slightly different versions of the decree were circulated.)

The preamble said, "We, the citizens of the State of Texas, County of Travis and City of Austin, by the providence of God, adhering to the Christian faith, having as our desire the glory of God and the advancement of the Kingdom of Our Lord and Savior Jesus Christ, as well as true public liberty, safety and peace; have resolved to enter into a mutual agreement with one another, before the most High God, to uphold the following truth. . . ."

The decree's conclusion said: "We further commit ourselves to support and encourage those elected officers and candidates who pledge to faithfully serve God in the administration of their office. We also solemnly warn that violation of such a sacred trust invites the judgment of God not only upon elect rulers, but also the communities which they represent and serve."

The state platform adopted a number of planks reflecting the Believers' Decree of Agreement, including a ban on the regulation of church schools, equal time for creationism in the classroom, an attack on "secular humanism" in the schools, a call for a quarantine of AIDS victims, a proposed Constitutional Amendment to elect federal judges every six years and force Supreme Court justices to retire at age eighty. But even while adopting many of the positions advanced in the Believers' Decree, the Texas GOP platform said, "The Republican Party of Texas does not require the endorsement of any particular 'Solemn Oath and Covenant' to participate in our party."

Religious Right groups were split in the gubernatorial race, with some backing Representative Tom Loeffler and some, including Robertson, backing former Representative Kent Hance; but former Republican governor William Clements, a moderate, won the nomination. Clements, however, later hired a "religious liaison" and wooed the Religious Right in his successful general election campaign. David Davidson, a Religious Right activist supported by the Texas Grassroots Coalition, won the nomination for lieutenant governor, but was defeated in the general election.

In the Fifth District, Tom Carter challenged Representative John Bryant, a Democrat. Pat Robertson sponsored a fund-raiser for Carter, who said, "We don't want a congressman who is rated 0 by Christian Voice for his opposition to family and moral issues."

In the Thirteenth District, Republican Beau Bolter, who won with Religious Right support in 1984, said he received "guidance from God on key issues facing Congress." He signed a Christian Voice fund-raiser and received money from Robertson's PAC.

Virginia

In the First District, a conservative Christian group called Peninsula Citizens for Freedom circulated a flyer which claimed that the Democratic challenger to Representative Herbert Bateman, State Senator Robert Scott, "has supported measures which definitively would have meant state control of certain religious activities." This district includes suburbs of Virginia Beach, Pat Robertson's home district.

In the Sixth District, Falwell's home district, Falwell and Robertson endorsed Flo Neher Traywick in her unsuccessful challenge to Representative James Olin.

TACTICS AND LEADERS

There were significant shifts in both tactics and leadership within the Religious Right in 1986. In the past, the Religious Right had been forthright in its goals; in 1986, however, there was outright deceit. The best example is a flyer on "How to Participate in a Political Party" distributed anonymously among Fundamentalists organizing within Republican county caucuses in Iowa. The flyer said,

The activities of the church must not become public knowledge. There are those who seek to undermine our work.

To a degree, keep your positions on issues to yourself. Jesus didn't overwhelm even his disciples with the truth—John 16:12. . . . Give the impression that you are there to work for the party, not to push an ideology. . . . Come across as being interested in economic issues. . . . Try not to let on that a close group of friends are becoming active in the party together.

Hide your strength. When you control a political party, the only times you want to show your strength is when 1. Electing officers; 2. Technically, when voting on resolutions, everyone votes his own conscience. . . . It is important not to clean house of all non-Christians. . . . When you have control of a party, it might not be wise to place "our" people into any and every position. Get the counsel of wise Christian politicians when in doubt.

In addition to advocating deceit, the flyer advocated something clearly contrary to the spirit of the First Amendment—using the political process to make religious conversions. The flyer advised, "Determine to win both friend and foe to the Lord. Don't do anything that will harm your testimony."

A flyer distributed anonymously in Republican caucuses in Minnesota said, "Experience has shown that it is best not to say you are entering politics because of Christian beliefs on life issues. It is better to say you favor the Republican Platform (it is pro-life) and support President Reagan. You will probably be asked outright if you are pro-life or pro-choice. Answer truthfully, or course. If the people asking this information are pro-choice, you can put them in a bad light by adding—'I am pro-life, but that is not the only issue.' "

Another shift involved the visibility of televangelists involved with the Religious Right. James Robison, highly visible in 1980 and in 1984, when he prayed at the Republican Convention, had a very low profile. Jimmy Swaggart, Tim LaHaye, and D. James Kennedy were less vocal on politics on their television programs, investing more of their time in related parts of the Religious Right agenda, attacking the courts and the public schools. LaHaye said on "Nightline," "Secular humanists should not hold political office in America. And the reason I say that is because our Constitution is not compatible with secular humanism without twisting it and changing it."

The biggest shift, however, involved Jerry Falwell and Pat Robertson. Up until 1986, Falwell had been the best-known and probably most influential Religious Right leader, while Robertson had concentrated more on his Christian Broadcasting Network (CBN). But while Falwell had been gathering media headlines, Robertson was putting together a political organization, and he dominated Religious Right activity in 1986.

In early 1986, Falwell announced that the Moral Majority would be subsumed by a broader, more political organization, the Liberty Federation. Two sociologists, Jeffey Hadden of the University of Virginia and Anson Shoupe of the University of Texas at Arlington, argued in a paper called, "Why Jerry Falwell Killed the Moral Majority," that the change was prompted by the fact that while the Moral Majority served to bring Falwell media attention, it was never a successful grassroots organization.

They noted that Falwell claimed the organization had 2 million to

3 million members. But, they said, the *Moral Majority Report* had a circulation of only 482,000. They also found that the Washington State executive director for Moral Majority said his chapter had 12,000 members, and the national office confirmed that that was the largest state organization. "Simple arithmetic," Hadden and Shoupe said, "led to the conclusion that the total size of the national organization had to be much smaller than Falwell was boasting."

Hadden and Shoupe studied the *Moral Majority Report* to look for evidence of local activity. They found "no evidence of sustained ongoing activities or projects that can be uniquely attributed to the Moral Majority." For example, they found that during 1984 and 1985, ten states reported no activity and eleven states reported only one activity; fourteen reported twice and only fifteen reported three or more times.

Hadden and Shoupe also found that half of all reported activities were in the Bible Belt, that only 38 percent were attributed to the Moral Majority alone and not to a coalition, and that 43 percent of the activities reported were in the future tense—they had not yet happened; furthermore, "we could not positively confirm that any of these projected activities actually happened."

Falwell even claimed that he was backing out of electoral politics. But he was still on record endorsing a number of candidates and his "I Love America Committee" PAC made contributions to candidates. On October 6, 1986, he sent out a fund-raising letter for the Liberty Federation which said, "You and I may be only a few weeks away from a national disaster—and for that reason—we have just launched a 'Thirty Day National Blitz'—a strategic action which we used very successfully in 1982. . . . [T]he liberals are already bragging that conservatives and pro-moral candidates will lose 30 seats in the House and—worst of all—that the liberals would take control of the Senate for the first time since 1980." Falwell said contributions would help him "launch a desperately needed campaign to reach hundreds of thousands of people right before the election" and "contact millions of voters by direct mail, television and radio."

While Falwell never made good on his pledge to withdraw from partisan politics, he was clearly eclipsed by Robertson, who launched a bid for the 1988 Republican presidential nomination and dominated Religious Right activity in 1986. Robertson was involved in a network of political organizations:

- The Committee for Freedom PAC.
- The Michigan Committee for Freedom PAC.
- The National Committee to Draft Pat Robertson for President, headed by Richard Minard, former director of Robertson's Freedom Council.
- The Pat Robertson for President Draft Committee, headed by Rob Flowe, former finance director for The Freedom Council.
- Robertson's own exploratory committee, Americans for Robertson.

But despite the existence of all these organizations, the most important Religious Right organization of 1986 was one which no longer exists—the Freedom Council. The council was disbanded after the Internal Revenue Service began investigating it and it refused to comply with Virginia registration laws.

The Freedom Council, a tax-exempt foundation, served as Robertson's de facto campaign organization. It organized local activity in Michigan, Iowa, Texas, New Hampshire, and other states and coordinated Robertson's visits to some twenty states. The Freedom Council described itself as "a nonprofit, nonpartisan Christian organization dedicated to reinforcing the traditional Judeo-Christian principles and values upon which the United States was founded. The council distributes practical political information through bible-believing churches and a growing bipartisan grassroots network. The council also maintains information bureaus in Washington, D.C., and in several state capitals to give local people a national and statewide perspective."

The council claimed 200,000 contributors, forty full-time field workers, and organizers in at least forty-one states. Robertson, who founded the council in 1981, said he no longer had any formal connection to it, but his actual control was obvious:

- Robertson's Christian Broadcasting Network contributed $250,000 a month to the council, accounting for half its budget.

- Robertson introduced a novel fund-raising technique at a May 16, 1986, dinner in Washington, D.C.: contributions ranged from $1,000 to $25,000 (for host couples). Because the limit on PAC contributions is $5,000, large donors gave their first $5,000 to the Committee for Freedom and the rest to the Freedom Council.

- The Freedom Council's original president, General Jerry Curry, resigned and was replaced on an interim basis by Bob Slosser, president of Christian Broadcasting Network University.

Robertson, who consulted with New Right leader Paul Weyrich about his candidacy drew heavily on people with connections to Weyrich to run the Freedom Council and his Committee for Freedom PAC:

- National field director Dick Minard was Northwest field director for Weyrich's Committee for the Survival of a Free Congress in 1979.

- James Ellis, assistant national director of the Freedom Council, is executive director of Weyrich's Free Congress Political Action Committee

- R. Marc Nuttle, president of the Committee for Freedom PAC, has been a consultant to the Committee for the Survival of a Free Congress.

The Freedom Council recruited thousands of candidates to run for delegate slots in Michigan, which selected some delegates in 1987 who will choose the presidential nominee in 1988.

Robertson was courted by the national Republican Party. He claimed to be "the third most prolific fund-raiser" for the party—presumably after President Reagan and Vice President Bush—and he accepted an invitation from the Republican Senatorial Campaign Committee to campaign for sixteen Senate candidates.

Robertson's campaign brought another practitioner of religious intolerance to the political forefront—televangelist Jimmy Swaggart, who initially opposed Robertson's running for president but was later pressured into an endorsement. Swaggart's religious intolerance easily earns him the title of "Robertson's Farrakhan": he has called

Catholicism a "false religion" and its teachings the "doctrine of devils"; he has called the Catholic Mass and mainline Protestant services "liturgical, religious monstrosities"; he has defended using scenes of the Holocaust to illustrate his belief that, "Whenever a person does not accept Jesus Christ, he takes himself away from God's protection. He then places himself under Satan's domain, who kills, steals, and destroys"; he has also condemned Mormonism and Christian Science.

THE BIBLICAL SCOREBOARD

A staple of religious intolerance on the part of the Religious Right has been a voting record or issues questionnaire which purports to measure candidates against the "Christian" or "biblical" positions on political issues. There is a very simple reason why claiming the correct "biblical" basis for a political position, like claiming God's endorsement, amounts to religious intolerance: it cuts off debate by arguing a position not on the basis of its political merits, but on the basis of religious authority. To do so demands that others accept—not tolerate, but consent to—the candidate's religious beliefs.

Some of those who have displayed religious intolerance or imposed a religious test on candidates have compounded the situation by claiming that critics are unfairly attacking or ridiculing their religion. In a sense, they try to have it both ways—cloaking their partisan political views in the garb of religion and appealing to religious tolerance as a defense.

As in 1984, a major source of religious intolerance in politics was the *Candidates Biblical Scoreboard,* compiled and distributed by Christian Voice and Biblical News Service. The *Scoreboard* contained a "disclaimer" saying it "is not intended, nor implied, to be a statistical judgment of a person's personal moral behavior or relationship with God." But the whole publication is based on the premise that Christian Voice knows the "biblical" position on current political issues based on a reading of selected passages from scripture; this style of debate constitutes religious intolerance and imposes a religious test for office.

The introduction to the *Scoreboard,* signed by Robert Grant of

Christian Voice and David Balsinger of Biblical News Service, added to the tone of religious intolerance:

The Christian exodus from political involvement during the past 85 years has left most of our government offices and institutions in the hands of amoral or immoral leaders. . . .

Although most political candidates claim a Judeo-Christian heritage, it's important to examine carefully their actual position on the biblical-family-moral-freedom issues. Their personal convictions on these issues will determine whether they lead our nation toward or away from Judeo-Christian values. . . .

By using our *Scoreboard* and voting for candidates who support Judeo-Christian values, you will be doing your Christian duty in helping to rebuild our nation and its institutions on the God-given foundation of Biblical truths."

The "biblical" positions stated in the *Scoreboard*—a dozen each in the House and Senate—include opposition to the Legal Services Corporation as an agent of "secular humanism"; support for the "Star Wars" defense plan; a balanced-budget constitutional amendment; opposition to "comparable worth" legislation; support for the Contras; and elimination of Library of Congress funding for a Braille edition of *Playboy.*

The *Scoreboard* took the words of the authors of the Old and New Testaments written for diverse audiences over a period of centuries and purported to find in them direct application to contemporary political issues. For example:

- The *Scoreboard* cited Genesis 2:18 ("And the Lord God said, 'It isn't good for man to be alone; I will make a companion for him, a helper suited to his needs' ") as the biblical basis for opposing the Equal Rights Amendment (ERA).

- It cited Galatians 5:1 ("It was for freedom that Christ set us free; therefore keep standing firm and do not be subjected again to the yoke of slavery") as the biblical basis for supporting military aid to the Contras in Nicaragua.

- It cited 2 Chronicles 19:2 ("Should you give hope to the wicked and love those who hate the Lord? Because of this, indignation shall come upon you") as the biblical basis for opposing trade with the Soviet Union.

- It cited Romans 1:28-30 ("So it was that when they gave God up and would not even acknowledge him, God gave them up to do everything their evil minds could think of. Their lives became fully of every kind of wickedness and sin. . . . They were backbiters, haters of God, insolent, proud braggarts, always thinking of new ways of sinning") as the biblical basis for opposing "secular humanism," which the Scoreboard found in the Legal Service Corporation.

As in the past, ministers in Congress did not score well on the *Biblical Scoreboard:* Senator John Danforth (R-Missouri), an Episcopal priest, received a 58 percent score, a "failing" grade; Representative Bob Edgar, a Methodist minister, and Representative William Gray, a Baptist minister—both Pennsylvania Democrats—scored 0.

Members of leading religious groups in general did not fare well: 107 of 140 Catholics in Congress failed; 32 of 38 Jews failed; 26 of 46 Baptists failed. Women and minorities did not fare well either: 15 of 19 women in congress failed; 10 of 11 Hispanics failed; all 20 blacks failed.

The *Scoreboard*'s partisanship was reflected in the fact that 36 of 53 Senate Republicans and 138 of 180 House Republicans passed, while 41 of 47 Senate Democrats and 227 of 255 House Democrats failed.

A variety of Religious Right and other conservative organizations distributed local versions of the *Scoreboard* in the closing weeks of the 1986 campaign. Christian Voice claims that 20 million copies of its *Scoreboard* were distributed:

- In California, Balsinger claimed to have distributed one million copies, with additional ratings of California Supreme Court justices up for election.
- In Colorado, Christian Voice, Concerned Women for America, Coalition on Revival, Colorado Citizens for Decency, Pro-Family Forum, Freedom's Quest, National Caleb Campaign, Morality in Media, and Christian Research Associates distributed local version of the *Scoreboard*.

- In Florida, televangelist D. James Kennedy sent copies of his own "Congressional Legislative Report," based on the Christian Voice *Scoreboard,* to his followers across the country.

- In Idaho, Christian Voice, Eagle Forum, Concerned Women for America, ACTV, Freedom Council, and Conservative Caucus distributed state versions of the *Scoreboard.*

- In Indiana, Christian Voice, the American Coalition for Traditional Values, and Americans for Biblical government distributed flyers attacking the voting records of Representatives Sharp, McCloskey, and Jacobs (10th District) as well as those of state candidates.

- In Louisiana, Jimmy Swaggart sent his followers in the state a local version of the *Scoreboard* in advance of the open primary in September.

- In south Dakota, Christian Voice, Eagle Forum, Christian Action Coalition, South Dakota Pro-Life, and South Dakota PSALM (People Serious About Liberty and Morality) distributed local versions of the *Scoreboard.*

QUESTIONNAIRES

Candidates' questionnaires are a common tool used by virtually every interest group in the country and as such are legitimate. Interest groups at both ends of the political spectrum circulate such questionnaires, and every candidate receives dozens of them to consider. But in recent years, a new type of questionnaire has emerged. These don't simply ask a candidate's position on Contra aid or abortion or even "secular humanism"; they ask questions about the candidate's belief in God, relationship to Jesus, or interpretation of the Bible.

Like the *Biblical Scoreboard,* these questionnaires constitute a form of religious intolerance; they are not designed to obtain information about political positions, but about religious beliefs which have no direct impact on political decisions. They clearly convey the impression that one type of religious belief is politically superior to others.

One organization clearly crossing the line was Pat Robertson's Freedom Council. Its branch in the 4th congressional district in

Georgia sent out a candidate questionnaire which asked, among other things, "Are you a Born-Again Christian?"; "Is Jesus Lord of Your Life?"; "Do you believe the Bible is the infallible Word of God?"

A cover letter signed by John Sauers, Vice Coordinator, said

We are concerned with our elected official's relationship to the God of the Bible which is also the same GOD of the Declaration of Independence, US Constitution, Pledge of Allegiance and all founding fathers of this great nation. We believe that our country needs to turn back to the basic Christian values which these God's men so clearly established in composition of our founding documents. We are not supporting any political party, but we are only seeking each candidate's spiritual beliefs with regard to the God of Abraham, Isaac, Jacob and Jesus Christ.

In Oklahoma, the Christian Action Coalition, composed of local offices of Christian Voice, Pat Robertson's Freedom Council, and Oklahomans Against Pornography distributed a questionnaire which asked candidates, "Do you believe that the basic premise of government and of the law is the Bible, rather than the word of any person?"

A questionnaire circulated in Sarasota, Florida, similarly crossed the line while reaching a new plateau in the use of the bible for partisan political ends. A group called "We the People" took out a full-page ad entitled "Election Guide: A Christian Perspective" in the *Sarasota Herald-Tribune*. The ad featured a questionnaire which asked such questions as, "Are you a Born-Again Christian?"

The ad said,

Many candidates stated they were Christians, but not born again. However, people use the term "Christian" in many different ways. Therefore, a "YES" answer to this question was limited to those individuals who said they were "born again" as discussed in the third chapter of the gospel of John. This question is asked to help voters know which candidates are dependent on God's Word for the wisdom necessary to make their public decisions. Non-Christians usually are limited to making their decisions based on their limited knowledge and common sense.

The "correct" answers to this questionnaire were based on Bible verses, including the "correct" responses to five questions related to the real estate business—"Are you in favor of government mandated rent controls (to protect the public) such as in mobile home parks?"—and purported to find a biblical basis for answers. (The correct answer to the rent control question is "No.") As it happens, the head of "We the People" is Scott Carver, president of Creative Reality company.

- In North Carolina, a group called Students for Better Government distributed a questionnaire asking "Can you honestly say that you have a personal relationship with Jesus Christ? How well do you know him?" and "If you answered 'Yes' . . . would you, if elected, seek God's guidance for your decisions? In no, how would you determine your answers and solutions?"

- In the 8th Congressional District in Indiana, the Rev. Donald Brooks of a Fundamentalist group called The Agora sent local and congressional candidates a questionnaire which included these questions: "If a regular church attender, how many times each month are you in attendance for a regular church service?"; "What is the name of your church and pastor?"; "Have you been or are your now a member of any group considered subversive, anti-God or anti-American?"; "In your opinion, is the Bible 1. A good book 2. A collection of religious writings 3. Literal, inerrant Word of God?"

- In Arizona, *Footprints,* a Fundamentalist newspaper distributed free in the Phoenix area, published a "Christian Voting Guide for Primary Election Sept. 9."

"PRAY FOR DEATH"

The year 1986 saw the emergence of the ultimate form of religious intolerance—Religious Right leaders praying for the death of Supreme Court justices and political officials with whom they disagreed. Pat Robertson stopped just short of doing this when he told the National Right to Life Committee meeting in Denver that abortion opponents could look to "the wonderful process of the mortality tables" to change the make-up of the court and bring about a new decision on abortion, in the same speech in which he called court members "despots."

For the first time, a major party congressional candidate joined the pray-for-death movement. The Rev. Joe Morecraft, a Fundamentalist pastor, John Birch Society member, and Republican nominee for the 7th District seat in Georgia, said on a local radio program that he prays for God to remove Supreme Court justices who support legal abortion "in any way he sees fit." Morecraft said, "I've prayed God would remove the Supreme Court justices of the United States Supreme Court who have consistently voted for the legalization of abortion on demand several times and I'll do it in the future, but I'll leave it to God to determine how he wants to do it."

The most detailed description of the "pray-for-death" approach comes from the Rev. Everett Sileven of Nebraska, who received national notoriety several years ago when he was jailed for refusing to comply with state regulations concerning a Christian school he ran. He became a cause celebre for the Religious Right; Jerry Falwell broadcast a program from Sileven's church.

Sileven, along with Indiana Moral Majority leader Rev. Greg Dixon and the Rev. Robert McCurry of Atlanta, has established a "Court of Divine Justice" in which they pray to God to "judge" public officials they consider "wicked rulers." Sileven has claimed that as a result of the "Courts of Divine Justice," a tornado hit the city of Fort Worth and the sheriff of the city was injured when his horse bucked and he came down on his saddlehorn; that a judge in Oregon had a heart attack; and that the son of a judge in Washington was seriously injured in an automobile accident. Sileven announced plans to hold a session of his "courts" on the steps of the US Supreme Court in the near future.

Sileven's partner, Greg Dixon, pastor of an eight-thousand-member church in Indianapolis, has a "Prayer hit list" of public officials condemned by his "Court of Divine Justice." In Austin, he prayed for the removal of office of Texas attorney general Jim Mattox "by whatever method, whether it be illness or whether it be death, whatever pleases God." Mattox says he has been harassed by late-night phone calls and has found a dead cat in front of his house.

There are other examples:

- The Rev. Robert Hymers of the Fundamentalist Baptist Church in downtown Los Angeles hired an airplane to carry a banner saying

"Pray for death: baby-killer Brennan" as Supreme Court Justice William Brennan, who in 1973 voted with the majority to legalize most abortions, was to deliver the commencement address at Loyola Marymount University. Hymers first gave out a press release saying his congregation would pray for Brennan's death; but, after deciding that would sound like "a lunatic fringe," Hymers merely prayed for Brennan's removal from the court.

But two weeks later, after the court upheld the right of a couple to withhold medical treatment from their handicapped daughter, Hymers prayed for the five justices in the majority—Marshall, Stevens, Blackmun, Powell, and Burger—to repent, retire, or die for their votes. "We will pray that God take the lives of these Hitler-like men from the face of the Earth," Hymers said.

- A group called Americans for Biblical Government, based in Hyattsville, Maryland, urged in its newsletter that members offer prayers "For the Supreme court—that either their minds be changed or that God would remove them and replace them with men who fear Him.

- The Rev. Tim LaHaye, head of the American Coalition for Traditional Values, said in a December 1985 newsletter that he was launching a national prayer campaign "for the removal (by any means God sees fit) of at least three of the Supreme Court members while Ronald Reagan is president."

The major danger of the "pray-for-death" movement was expressed succinctly by Rev. Hymers himself when he backed off of his prayer for the death of Justice Brennan—"we don't want to put into someone's mind that they should go out and kill him." But that is exactly what Hymers and others have done. By using the same kind of inflammatory rhetoric some in the Religious Right used before the outbreak of bombings at abortion clinics, they run the risk of inciting an unbalanced follower to attempt to do what they think is God's will by trying to kill a public official with whom they disagree.

ELECTION RETURNS

When the 1986 election returns were in, the Religious Right had suffered a number of setbacks, in particular, losing some of its most vocal supporters in the Senate. One election does not destroy a movement, however—there are still more than one hundred members of Congress with a 90 percent or better rating from Christian Voice. But new and highly visible Religious Right candidates did not do well in 1986.

For example, eight of the surviving members of the Senate Class of 1980 had been elected with strong Religious Right support; four were defeated in their bids for reelection—Jeremiah Denton of Alabama, Paula Hawkins of Florida, Mack Mattingly of Georgia, and James Abdnor of South Dakota. Of the winners, Dan Quayle of Indiana never faced a serious challenge; Don Nickles of Oklahoma had a surprisingly easy race again Representative James Jones; Steve Symms of Idaho won a close race against Governor John Evans, and Robert Kasten of Wisconsin won a surprisingly close race over former National Football League Player Representative Ed Garvey. (Another senator elected in 1980, Charles Grassley of Iowa, was elected with Religious Right support, but moved away from the movement and the administration on issues like the M-X missile and military spending, and was reelected with a broad base of support.)

All four Religious Right Senate candidates running for the first time were defeated. The most significant race involved James Broyhill, who had been appointed to the Senate to replace the late Senator John East of North Carolina, a close ally of Jesse Helms. Broyhill had turned back a challenge from a Religious Right candidate in the primary, but embraced the movement in his general campaign and was defeated by former governor Terry Sanford. The next most significant race was in Colorado where Representative Ken Kramer, a Jewish supporter of Christian Voice, lost to Democratic representative Tim Wirth after Christian Voice became a campaign issue. Two other Religious Right candidates—Tom Kindness in Ohio and Asa Hutchinson in Arkansas—lost as expected in challenges to John Glenn and Dale Bumpers.

The Religious Right members of the House Class of 1984 did considerably better—eight of ten were reelected. The winners were Robert Dornan of California, Pat Swindall of Georgia, Bill Hendon of North Carolina, and five Texans—Joe Barton, Beau Bolter, Mac Sweeney, Larry Combest, and Richard Armey. The two losses came in swing districts in North Carolina as William Cobey and William Coble were defeated. Cobey's defeat was particularly significant be- cause of his charge that his opponent "is not willing to take a strong stand for the principles outlined in the Word of God." Another Religious Right leader, Mark Siljander of Michigan, was defeated in the Republican primary in the Fourth Congressional District after he said his victory was needed "to break the back of Satan."

New Religious Right candidates running for House seats did poorly in 1986. Only one—Jim Inhofe, former mayor of Tulsa, Oklahoma, and local Freedom Council coordinator—was elected. The most significant defeat involved James Butcher, who defeated an establishment Republican candidate in the primary but lost to a Democrat in a race for an open seat in a heavily Republican district, the Fifth Congressional District in Indiana. Other losers were Rob Scribner in California; Mary Collins in Florida; Joe Morecraft in Georgia; William Costas, Donald Lynch, and Richard McIntyre in Indiana; Jackie McGregor in Michigan; Dale Bell in South Dakota; Jim Golden in Tennessee; and Tom Carter in Texas.

The 1986 midterm elections provided a number of further lessons about the relationship of religion and politics in America.

1. Religion continues to be a major factor in political life in a variety of ways—from the Religious Right's efforts to take over the Republican Party to the Democratic Party's mishandling of the religion issue; belief in religions ranging from Transcendental Meditation to Christian Science became issues in 1986.

2. When political participation is low, particularly in caucuses or low turn-out primaries, the influence of fringe groups, whether the Religious Right or LaRouche adherents, is magnified and can affect the whole political system.

3. Given sufficient information and a choice, the American people will reject both religious intolerance and partisan appeals to religion.

4. The Religious Right suffered a setback, but remains a major factor in American politics. Once its followers are elected, it is not easy to unseat them.

5. Both religious intolerance and partisan appeals to religion are being institutionalized within the Republican Party. The Republicans appealed to Evangelicals at the local, state, and national levels on the basis of their belief in a "personal relationship with Christ" and to Jews on the basis of the Jewishness of a candidate's spouse or children. Both approaches threaten the spirit of the First Amendment and strike at the heart of the American belief in religious tolerance and pluralism.

6. Pat Robertson: Extremist with a Baby Face

"I'm not really on the Religious Right, whatever that is," Pat Robertson told *The Sunday Oklahoman* in early 1987. "I'm mainstream."

In his quest for the 1988 Republican presidential nomination, the former televangelist and host of the "700 Club" TV show sought to minimize his religious connections and paint himself as a mainstream Republican; when the Jim and Tammy Bakker scandal broke, for example, a spokesman for Robertson said he was a broadcaster, not an "evangelist." *The New Republic* called Robertson the "Teflon Televangelist" because criticism had not stuck to him. Robertson was indeed lucky—he had visibility, but not exposure. After Robertson's strong showing in early Michigan caucuses to choose delegates for the 1988 Republican Convention, media coverage moved quickly to the horse-race stage, focusing on Robertson's strength and potential impact on the choice of the 1988 Republican presidential nominee. That was even more the case when Robertson shocked political observers by winning a Republican straw ballot in Iowa in September 1987.

Robertson's image also benefited from association with others in the public arena: former President Jimmy Carter was a born-again Christian; Jesse Jackson is a Baptist minister; President Reagan is a conservative. Finally, Robertson's personal manner—smooth, polished, smiling, reassuring—is not threatening.

All of these factors have combined to obscure the fact that Pat Robertson is an extremist whose views place him well outside the mainstream of both the Republican Party and the nation. At one level, Robertson offers the extremism of the Religious Right, with its claims of a divinely mandated political agenda. At another level, he offers views long associated with secular right-wing extremists.

Robertson's record deserves careful scrutiny to reveal in depth the thinking of a man who, despite his disclaimers, represents the heart of the Religious Right in America and who was treated as a serious presidential candidate by the Republican Party. Robertson resigned his ministry in the Southern Baptist Convention just before formally announcing his candidacy on October 1, 1987, in order to deflect criticism of his religious agenda. But it was not Robertson's ordination that upset people—it was his ideas.

Robertson is quick to equate criticism of himself with prejudice against ministers or Evangelicals becoming involved in the political process. That tactic is typical of his smearing of those who disagree with him with labels like "atheist" and "Communist." When People for the American Way issued a report criticizing Robertson's views, he responded by calling Norman Lear an "atheist," claiming that the organization "wants to move us towards a collectivist, socialistic model" and warning his followers that "God's people have to understand that the enemy is the Father of Lies"—Satan.

Robertson compared concern raised by his candidacy to that which initially faced John F. Kennedy when he sought to become the nation's first Catholic president. But the analogy does not hold up. Kennedy campaigned to show that he could be president of all Americans. In contrast, Robertson described his early success in the Michigan caucuses this way in a fund- raising letter for the Freedom Council: "The Christians have won! . . . What a thrust for freedom! What a breakthrough for the Kingdom! . . . As believers become involved in this process, they will be able to turn the nation back to its traditional moral values." In sharpening his distinction between "the Christians" and everyone else, Robertson proclaimed in Michigan that Christians—meaning only born-again Christians—"maybe feel more strongly than others do" about "love of God, love of country and support for the traditional family."

Robertson has spoken repeatedly as though Fundamentalists hold a privileged position in America:

- "We Christians are using what is ours and we're going to bring back righteousness to this land" (Mesa, Arizona, *Tribune,* March 15, 1987).

- Robertson claimed that the Supreme Court has rendered Christians "a persecuted minority in our own land" (*Miami Herald,* April 12, 1987).
- He said on the "700 Club" on October 13, 1986, "A person who is not born again cannot enter into Heaven. We're talking about millions of people! And you say, 'Well, you shouldn't interfere with their lifestyle. They're going to do their thing.' Well, maybe they're going to do their thing, but their thing is a broadway to destruction. That's what Jesus Christ told us. And he came to give us a Christian country."

Robertson's language on these occasions disturbed even fellow Evangelicals. Senator Bill Armstrong (R-Colorado) said "Evangelicals should never, never give the impression that in pressing their opinion . . . they are somehow speaking with authority of scripture or church or God." He said they make a "horrible mistake" if they do so: "For Christians to step across the line and try to assume for the church a role of being power brokers or being a power block is not only being untruthful to the faith, but it invites a backlash, and properly so."

PAT'S PIPELINE TO GOD

Before formally announcing his candidacy, Robertson said he was waiting for God to tell him whether or not to run; as he moved toward announcing, he said that God had told him to run. Given his history, it is not surprising that he put it that way; for almost a quarter of a century, Robertson has claimed to receive detailed answers from God to problems in his professional life.

The pages of Robertson's first book, *Shout It From the Rooftops* (1972), are full of references to God's involvement in the early days of Robertson's broadcasting career. Robertson told the owner of a small TV station he wanted to buy, "God has sent me here to buy your television station. . . . God's figure is $37,000, and the station has to be free from all debts and encumbrances."

Robertson also wrote about an early "700 Club" program. After speaking for about an hour, he was about to invite members of the audience to accept Christ: "After the third sentence, God spoke, 'This is not the time.' " Robertson says he introduced a young singing group and that after they sang, God said "Now."

According to Robertson, God even kept him from campaigning for his father, Senator A. Willis Robertson, in the 1966 Democratic primary in which he was defeated. "I yearned to get into the fray and start swinging, but the Lord refused to give me the liberty. 'I have called you to my ministry,' he spoke to my heart. 'You cannot tie my eternal purposes to the success of any political candidate . . . not even your own father.' " (This passage was missing from a 1987 reprint of *Shout It From the Rooftops;* spokesmen for Robertson denied that he was responsible.)

Robertson is not shy about identifying himself with God's purpose: "The start of construction of our (Christian Broadcasting Network [CBN]) headquarters building on the same day that the Six-Day War began was highly significant. The takeover of Jerusalem by the Jews during that war was a signal that the times of the Gentiles had ended. In my thinking, the ministry of CBN was an end-time ministry. Like John the Baptist, we had been called to proclaim the end of the old age and to prepare the people for the coming of Jesus Christ and the new age."

Robertson continued his chronicle of god's interest in CBN in a later book, *The Secret Kingdom* (1982). According to Robertson, God provided helpful investment tips: "I was praying one day in 1969, and the Lord spoke plainly to my inner man: 'The stock market is going to crash.' This was startling, for I hadn't even been thinking about the stock market. Then he added: 'Only the securities of your government will be safe.' "

Robertson claimed that God also made a CBN telethon a success:

I was speaking in prophecy about the presence of the Lord in what we were doing, and then the word of wisdom came regarding the telethon several days thence: "It will be so marvelous that you will not believe that it is happening. And yet this is going to happen before your eyes; and when it does happen, do not give credit to yourself, to your program people, to your computer operators, or to any of the things that you have done. But give Me credit because I am telling you now that I am going to do it. And when it's over, you will see it and you will know who did it."

Of course, the word was fulfilled and we dramatically exceeded our goal. He met our need and the need of the people we were ministering to.

Robertson also wrote that God told him to buy land for the site of CBN University: " 'I want you to buy the land,' the Lord said. 'Buy it all,' He said. 'I want you to build a school there for My glory, as well as the headquarters building you need.' "

In his book *Beyond Reason: How Miracles Can Change Your Life* (1984), a "how-to" book about working miracles, Robertson, who claims to be a faith-healer, said that during the 1960s, God turned a hurricane away from Virginia Beach to spare the CBN tower and has kept the area free of hurricanes ever since: "As I prayed out loud . . . faith rose within me, and with authority in my voice, I found myself speaking to a giant, killer hurricane about one hundred miles away in the Atlantic Ocean. Specifically, I commanded that storm, in the name of Jesus, to stop its forward movement and to head back where it had come from." Robertson says the hurricane stopped in its tracks at the precise time he had commanded it to stop and later made a 180-degree turn. "Skeptics may offer other explanations for these events. But I know it was God's power that spared this region and also CBN's tower."

Robertson continued to claim to speak for God. On November 3, 1982, just before Election Day, Robertson said on the "700 Club" that he had been praying for the election of senatorial candidates Pete Wilson in California and Paul Trible in Virginia and that he had a "peaceful feeling" about the races. His cohost, Ben Kinchlow, pointed out that both candidates were Republicans and said, "It sounds, for example, that somebody could be sitting out there now, saying: 'Well, now, I didn't have a chance, there's no way I could win my race in California or Virginia, if God is Republican." Robertson answered,

God isn't Republican. It's just in these two particular races. I'm not so sure God gets into these things. I remember years ago, praying for one particular presidential candidate and the Lord said: "Don't pray." And I said "Why not?" And He said "The people don't want him. They don't want what he stands for. Period. End of story." And then the Lord showed me also that this person wasn't the great person that we had all hoped he was anyhow. That he wasn't sweetness and light to begin with. . . . So the Lord, I think, may give us wisdom of what's going to happen, but he isn't saying: "I'm going to be out there changing things, necessarily, in every race." He has [gotten] in who he wants, but in a free society, apparently, he allows people to do what they want to do.

But Robertson claimed a direct link between God and the Republican Party in a 1986 rally in Jackson, Mississippi, claiming that God responded to the first Washington for Jesus rally: "On April 25, 1980, 500,000 Christians gathered on the mall in Washington and prayed that God would please heal our land. It was no coincidence that Ronald Reagan was elected president; it was the direct act of God, and that Strom Thurmond became head of the [US Senate] Judiciary Committee rather than Teddy Kennedy. The Republican takeover and reversal of direction in this country is no coincidence." (*Jackson News,* June 3, 1986).

Robertson also claimed to speak for God on political issues in an August 5, 1985, fund-raising letter for the Freedom Council Foundation. Robertson attacked the Supreme Court's decision to strike down a school prayer "moment of silence" law in Wallace v. Jaffree. Robertson said, "Once again the will of God—and the will of the American people—has been thwarted by a handful of misguided individuals."

In the same letter, he said "We must arise and exercise our responsibility before God to assert dominion on earth. I am certain that as we take authority in His name, God will raise up champions from among His people— individuals who, like David of old, will run out to do battle with the taunting Goliaths of secularism who are oppressing God's people, and lead others in the battle for our spiritual liberties."

The theme of God's people taking authority has become more common in Robertson's "700 Club" appearances since he launched his presidential campaign. For example, on May 1, 1986, he said, "God's plan, ladies and gentlemen, is for his people to take dominion. . . . What is dominion? Dominion is Lordship. He wants His people to reign and rule with Him."

On May 16, he said, "The Evangelicals [are] a force that nobody else really has been reckoning with, but they're going to be one to be reckoned with because God is establishing this. . . . God is going to be prospering but the intention of the Lord that his people should reign and rule with Jesus Christ. That's what the bible says."

Robertson identified himself with God's will in a 1981 letter to People for the American Way. Robertson protested the group's successful effort to get air time to challenge his statement on the "700 Club" that federal judges "exercise what amounts to a form of dictatorship." Robertson wrote: "Though I am a former Golden Gloves boxer, I dislike fights. I seldom fight, but when I do, I seldom lose. But regardless of my personal action, I want to warn you with all solemnity in the words of the old Negro spiritual, 'Your arms are too short to box with God.' The suppression of the voice of God's servant is a terrible thing! God himself will fight for me against you—and He will win!"

Robertson was asked about this quote on "Meet the Press" (December 15, 1985). Correspondent Robert Abernathy added, "I want to ask you about tolerance. If you were in public office, could you give up that attitude?"

Robertson replied,

When a person is talking about a budget bill, that's a temporal matter. It's a question of what do you spend your money on, how do you allocate money. When you're talking about a foreign trade bill, when you're talking about tax bills, the basic issue is not God's will or man's will. The issue is, Is this a smart move or isn't it? It's not a question of being conservative or liberal, but is it smart or is it foolish? And—however, when you're talking about eternal verities, and someone tries to take you off the air, for example, the term prophet in our culture means someone who addresses social ills. It means somebody who speaks for God. It's not some sort of spooky thing . . .

While Robertson tried to put his comments in a better light, what he was saying was clear—when it comes to the "eternal verities," Pat Robertson speaks for God.

On the same "Meet the Press" program, Robertson also elaborated on what he means by saying he is waiting for God to tell him whether to run for president. "Well," he said, "there are a number of ways that God speaks to people. He speaks through circumstances. He speaks through study of the Bible. He speaks through the advice of friends, and he speaks primarily through an inner peace that people get that what they're doing is right and proper, and all those things can come together and a person can say, well, I feel this is the will of God for me."

In several other interviews, Robertson listed some of the people he is talking to to determine God's will for him: They include Jerry Falwell; Tim LaHaye, head of the American Coalition for Traditional Values (ACTV); Bill Bright, head of the Campus Crusade for Christ; Charles Stanley and Jimmy Draper, Fundamentalists who are former presidents of the Southern Baptist Convention; former Reagan aide Ed Rollins; and New Right leader Paul Weyrich. It seems, then, that God may be Republican—and a right-wing Republican—after all.

Robertson further elaborated on his efforts to determine God's will for his political future in a remarkable interview with a "700 Club" reporter on June 11, 1986, in which Robertson referred to his claim that his prayer had turned Hurricane Gloria, which was headed for Virginia Beach, out to sea in 1985:

Q: How important was Hurricane Gloria in this crystalization process?
Robertson: Well, it was extremely important because I felt, interestingly enough, that if I couldn't move a hurricane, I could hardly move a nation. I know that's a strange thing for anybody to say, and there's hardly anyone else who would feel the same way, but it was very important to the faith of many people. . . .
Q: If it had come ashore, would you have seen that as a signal from the Lord not to "go for it"?
Robertson: Absolutely. I would have done a Sherman the next morning.

Q: Some people think [running] would be a step down. . . .
Robertson: I would only do it [run for president] if I felt it was a direct call and leading of God and it was something he told me I had to do and I would do it under those circumstances.
Q: Does that mean that anyone who opposes you is opposed to God?
Robertson: Absolutely not. Everybody has to make his own decisions. I

couldn't run as "God's candidate" or say that I was the moral man and some-body else was immoral. I would have to stand on issues. I think it would be arrogant and unfair to come out and say, "Well, I'm God's anointed." I wouldn't want anybody else to say that, and I certainly wouldn't do it myself.

Robertson continues to talk about the hurricane which he still be-lieves he moved. On C-SPAN on April 27, 1987, he described a con-versation with Phil Donahue:

"I said, 'Phil, a hurricane was coming down on my city that would have done millions of dollars worth of damage to life and property and I asked God, along with about a million other people, that it might not hit us and would go out to sea.' The thing of it is, it went out to sea, and that is the uncontrovertible fact. The newspaper in our home community said we were lucky. I say it was answer to pray-er. So, I will continue to say that, because everything I can read in the Bible, and from past history, indicates that God indeed does answer prayer, and he does it in relation to storms and the weather."

Robertson has added a new twist to his hurricane story: "Sixteen people were killed when the storm turned up the coast and plowed into New England and New York. What, Robertson was asked, would he tell the families of those 16? 'Maybe you should ask Mario Cuomo and Ed Koch why they didn't pray,' he grinned, then turned away" (*San Francisco Chronicle,* July 20, 1987).

If anything, Robertson became even more vocal in claiming God's endorsement as his campaign progressed. "Do I know the will of God? Of course I do" (Manchester, New Hampshire *Sunday News,* July 26, 1987).

He even fit Gary Hart's initial withdrawal from the race into God's plan for his own election. The *Fresno Bee* on July 19, 1987, reported that "To campaign workers, Robertson cited Gary Hart's abrupt de-parture from the campaign and George Bush's loss of support in the polls. He then talked of God's leading him to run for the presidency and of God's leading in 1959, when he began the Christian Broad-casting Network with $70. Robertson was asked if he sensed God at work in creating an open presidential race where he now has a chance. 'I'll let you draw your own conclusions,' he replied, adding: 'If there was a strong front-runner, I wouldn't be a candidate. I not only have a chance, I'm going to win the nomination and the election.' "

Robertson's denial that he claims to be God's candidate was good politics and good theology; but, unfortunately, it was just not credible. Robertson repeatedly claimed to have a direct pipeline to God; he said God wanted him to run; and he looks for God's voice in the words of right-wing politicians; he told his viewers that God wants his people to take dominion; he claimed to have worked a miracle and that having done so will figure in his decision to run for president.

History shows that Americans like their presidents to pray. That attitude does not reflect mere piety; it has a very practical dimension as well. Presidents who pray and feel awed by God's power presumably have a strong sense of humility that will keep them and the nation out of trouble. Robertson's history clearly shows that he has no real sense of humility and that, convenient denials aside, he sees no difference between God's will and his own personal ambitions.

ROBERTSON'S TWO VIEWS OF CHURCH-STATE SEPARATION

The question of whether or not Pat Robertson has a personal pipeline to God is not the only issue on which Robertson can argue both sides; he is also considerably at odds with himself on the meaning of the separation of church and state. On one hand, Robertson tells mainstream media outlets that he supports the separation of church and state; but when he talks to his "700 Club" audience or conservative outlets, he takes a much different line, attacking the separation of church and state as an "atheistic Communist" idea.

When in his moderate mode, Robertson can speak eloquently about the separation of church and state. "The president . . . is the president of all the people," he told the *USA Today* editorial board (July 1, 1986). "He has, not the power of persuasion, he has the power of the sword—he can tax them, he can force compliance. And it's a totally different matter." He said on "Meet the Press" that, if elected president, he would not try to use the power of his office to convert

Americans to Christianity. Asked on the program, "You do believe in the separation of church and state, do you not?" he replied "Certainly."

Robertson, however, has repeatedly tried to undermine separation by claiming that the US Constitution says nothing about the separation of church and state, but that the phrase appears in the Soviet Constitution. For example, on the "700 Club" (September 30, 1981), he claimed that after the Soviet Constitution was written, a new doctrine came into being in 1920 with the creation of the American Civil Liberties Union (ACLU); that doctrine, he said, was designed to remove religion from American life and to bring US policy in line with that of the Soviet Union.

In 1984, Robertson even commissioned a Gallup Poll asking Americans to identify which statement appears in the US Constitution—the First Amendment ("Congress shall make no law respecting an establishment of religion or prohibiting the free exercise thereof") or "The state shall be separate from the church and church from state," which he said was from the Soviet Constitution (Robertson paraphrased the Soviet Constitution; 55 percent correctly identified the First Amendment).

The implications of the First Amendment for a wide variety of public policy and individual rights issues have been hotly debated for decades. But it is clear that the constitutional ban on governmental establishment of religion means, at the very least, that public officials cannot govern by purporting to find specific laws and policies in biblical quotes. It has been legitimate in American history to cite the Bible in support of general principles, but the reason it cannot be used as a legal code is obvious—not all Americans accept the Bible as God's word, and there is considerable difference in interpretation among those who do.

Robertson, however, has on a number of occasions described government as an arm of religion and argued for certain public policies not on the basis of their merits, but on the basis that he finds them in the Bible:

- He claims that "our form of government came directly from the Bible" ("700 Club," August 20, 1984) and that "the early laws of the country reflected the teachings of Jesus Christ, and the teachings of Paul, as recorded in the Bible" ("700 Club" January 24, 1983).

- Robertson says the only way to reduce the national budget deficit is to follow biblical guidance: "The debt is what the problem is . . . and every fifty years, God said 'Let's declare a Year of Jubilee, cancel all the debts and get on with it.' But we don't follow God's way and so we get caught on this hook again." ("700 Club," May 28, 1982); "God's way is every fifty years to have a Jubilee and cancel all the debts . . . that is the only way to solve the recession and national debt." ("700 Club," July 15, 1982).

- In 1984, he said, "We're asking for Godly people to be in office. We're praying particularly in this election you want men of God in various levels of life . . . men and women who love God, who believe in the Bible . . ." ("700 Club")

- He told *Time* magazine (February 17, 1986) that one reason he was considering running for president was because of his concern about the question, as he framed it, "Would the government as such choke off a moral renewal if certain tendencies that have been evident in past administrations were brought back?"

- In *USA Today*, June 27, 1986, Robertson said he supports the death penalty because, "The judicial execution of a rebel against society has never been forbidden by the Bible."

- In responding to a fund-raising letter signed by Democratic National Committee Chairman Paul Kirk which criticized Robertson for saying that wives must be submissive to their husbands, Robertson cited Ephesians 5 and said, "For the first time in the history of America, as far as I know, a major political party has now begun an attack on the Bible itself. Paul Kirk . . . called the views of the Apostle Paul concerning the role of women in marriage appalling. Now, that is shocking, you say, that one party would actually come out and say in essence, 'We are going to support initiatives which would go contrary to the Christian view of marriage,' and yet such a letter was written and publicized widely . . ." ("700 Club," May 19, 1986).

Once again, Robertson put a different face on an issue for *USA*

Today when he said of his biblical view of the nature of marriage "things like that cannot be said or even considered in the context of politics, because it's a totally different arena."

- Robertson told *Time* (February 17, 1986), "The prophet Isaiah says we are supposed to lift the yoke of oppression. . . . Pacifism is not biblical. We have to realize that we are dealing with a malevolent power that over the last four decades has resulted in the death of over 250 million human beings. There has never been a force in the history of the world that has been as vicious, as malevolent, and at its core, atheistic and desirous of destroying the liberties of people. I think that if we have the opportunity to assist these wars of liberation, as in Afghanistan or Nicaragua or Angola, we should do that. We have no obligation to assist the enemies of the US or the enemies of the Lord or the enemies of freedom."

- In the same interview, Robertson related his view of the Middle East and the possibility of the Soviet Union moving against Israel to the Bible: "This is the most volatile area in the whole world, and if you read the Bible, it seems to be considered the center of the Earth. . . . If they [the Soviet Union] begin a venture in the Middle East as I read the Bible, God is going to bring it to pass, not America or anybody else."

It is clear that Robertson pays lip service to "the separation of church and state" while simultaneously trying to cloud the concept as a communistic notion. It is also clear that he finds justifications for specific public policy options in the Bible in a manner that is clearly contrary to the traditional American concept of church-state separation because it would form public policy on the basis of sectarian doctrine.

ARMAGEDDON THEOLOGY

Robertson's reference in the *Time* interview to biblical prophecies about the Middle East stem from his belief in "Armageddon theology," a form of Fundamentalism which holds that the Bible offers a detailed prophetic description of events—including war in the Middle East—leading to the Second Coming of Christ and the end of the world. Armageddon theology has long been the backbone of Robertson's religious belief system. He sketched out the Armageddon theology scenario in his book *The Secret Kingdom* (1982):

"Various people have been viewed as Gog and Magog throughout history—the Goths, the Cretans, the Scythians—but indications are that this great power from the north may be the Soviet Union, for that nation occupies land specified by Ezekiel. Other present-day nations that we seem to identify in the confederation are Ethiopia, Iran as Persia, Somalia or Libya as Put and Eastern Europe (probably Germany) as Gomer. It is noteworthy that Iran, at this writing, is mounting a crusade to "liberate" Jerusalem and is drawing near to the Soviet Union. Ethiopia is a communist dictatorship; Libya tilts toward Moscow; and Somalia, although leaning toward the United States, has been Marxist. East Germany, a Soviet satellite, has positioned police forces in South Yemen and other parts of the Middle East. Thus, the various pieces of Ezekiel's prophecy appear to be easing into place . . . .

At the same time, the Book of Revelation appears to point to a successor kingdom to the Roman Empire that could roughly parallel the current European Economic Community. It could be a forerunner of what is called the Antichrist. Presumably the group will make a league with Israel and then turn on her and begin to oppress her.

Robertson returned to this scenario in *Answers to 200 of Life's Most Probing Questions* (1984). He points to the centrality of the creation of the state of Israel in 1948 and its recapture of the city of Jerusalem in 1967 as the fulfillment of important parts of biblical prophecy about the Second Coming of Christ. Robertson downplays one part of Armageddon theology emphasized by other Fundamentalist leaders—the belief that all Jews will either convert or be killed during a seven-year Tribulation period. But he does say that "those who refuse to accept Christ will grow worse and worse in their wickedness. It will become increasingly difficult for the church and the world to coexist."

Other signs of Christ's return, Robertson says, include an increase in sinfulness and an explosion of knowledge.

Add to this the ability of computers to monitor the behavior of populations and to control all of the world's money. These developments are fulfilling biblical prophecies. This tells me that we are getting very close to the time when God is going to say that the human race has gone far enough. He may be ready to step in to terminate this phase of human activity and to start another one.

That is why I firmly expect to be alive when Jesus Christ comes back to Earth.

Armageddon theology also involves a belief in numerology. Robertson says in *Answers*, "In the Book of Revelation there is reference to the number of the Antichrist, which is 666. . . . Six is the number of man, whereas seven is the number of perfection. So 666 may refer to the quintessential humanist. Revelation tells us that the number 666 is going to be stamped upon the hand and the forehead of every person in the world during the reign of the Antichrist." Robertson says the use of microchips in "smart" credit cards and the coming of electronic fund transfers "could easily fulfill what Revelation says: that people could not buy or sell without the mark of the Beast."

Robertson has discussed Armageddon theology in detail on the "700 Club." On December 3, 1981, Ben Kinchlow asked, "Does the Bible specifically tell us what is going to happen in the future?" Robertson replied, "It sure does, Ben. . . . [I]t specifically, clearly, unequivocally [says] . . . that Russia and other countries will enter into war and God will destroy Russia through earthquakes, volcanoes, etc." After the Israeli invasion of Lebanon in 1982, Robertson predicted a Soviet-led invasion of Israel that could put the world "in flames" by the end of the year and lead to the Second Coming by the year 2000 (*Newsweek*, July 5, 1982). On May 20, 1982, Robertson said, "The Bible says that . . . the Soviet Union is going to make a move against this little nation known as Israel. And that's got to happen because it is very clear cut in the Bible in the last days; and along with the Soviet Union there is going to be Iran, there is going to be Ethiopia, possibly Libya, some East German forces which are now in South Yemen, this is going to happen. . . . [T]here is going to be a move by the Soviet Union into the Middle East."

The Wall Street Journal (October 17, 1985) reported, "[Robertson] says he no longer believes—as he once told his followers—that the Bible predicts a nuclear war and the beginning of the end of the world in the 1980s."

Robertson was even flip in talking about Armageddon theology in a May 5, 1987, interview with the Concord, New Hampshire, *Monitor:* " 'In the late '70s under Jimmy Carter, a lot us of thought the end was near,' he said, laughing. He didn't feel like getting serious about those days, especially since a man runs for president to shape the future, not preside over its terminus. 'Other than that, I'd rather not say, but I do think that I'm more optimistic. Possibly I was a little off in my assumptions in terms of the imminent demise of society.' "

But flip remarks are not persuasive in the face of massive details about Robertson's belief in Armageddon theology—a belief spelled out as recently as 1984 in *Answers*.

That is important, because Armageddon theology clearly has political implications. The greatest danger it presents is a disdain for peace, particularly in the Middle East. Robertson was particularly pessimistic about the prospects for peace in the wake of the Israeli invasion of Lebanon. "There's not going to be any peace until God's peace, what we call the peace of Jerusalem, when the Prince of Peace brings peace to that troubled region. . . . And any peace initiatives are going to be frustrated, we're afraid, over those intervening few months and years." ("700 Club," October 18, 1982).

Robertson's disdain for peace extends to the Soviet Union, which, as an "atheistic, humanistic" empire is clearly linked to the power of Satan in his worldview. The practical implications of Robertson's belief in Armageddon theology are apparent in his comments on the 1985 US-Soviet summit:

In my view, we will never achieve anything meaningful with the Soviet Union unless it will be to their benefit. And they will not keep any treaty that does not benefit them . . . because lying, according to Lenin, is part of their strategy. And they don't mind lying in written documents. If it's to their benefit to keep the agreements then they'll do it, but basically speaking, their mindsets is one of deceit and harassment and oppression. Ours is one of openness and truthfulness and from the Judeo-Christian point of view. We come at these things from totally different cultures, totally different mindsets and I personally don't think anything meaningful is going to come out of it" ("700 Club," November 15, 1985).

Robertson's increasingly bellicose rhetoric during his campaign suggests that he still views the Soviet Union as satanic. "I want to see as a foreign policy of the United States of America the ultimate elimination of communism in all the nations of the world, including the Soviet Union" (Mesa, Arizona, *Tribune,* March 29, 1987); "We should urge as the policy of the United States the ultimate downfall of communism in every nation in the world, including the Soviet Union" (*Atlanta Constitution,* March 17, 1987).

Robertson suggested that America "roll back" communism in Angola, Mozambique, Afghanistan, Ethiopia, and Nicaragua. "The Soviets know that if they take one from us, we have the perfect right to take one back from them. As we begin to unravel their empire, then the nation ultimately will begin to go. As long as it seems that communism, or at least Russian expansionism, is the wave of the future, the nations will be afraid to resist it. But if the United States is strong, and we support the armies of liberation in the countries I mentioned, I think we can see the ultimate unraveling of communism of its own way. It will fall of its own way if we won't support it" (Swartz Creek, Michigan, *West Valley News,* March 22, 1987).

Robertson also resorted to vintage McCarthyism in trying to portray his critics as procommunist: "I think that we as Republicans should dedicate ourselves to freedom. And if the other party along the way wants to align itself with the Brezhnev Doctrine, to make the world safe for Communist aggression, that's their business" (Spartanburg, South Carolina, *Herald-Journal,* April 5, 1987).

Robertson's belief in Armageddon theology shapes his rejection of peace efforts in the Middle East and arms control negotiations with the Soviet Union. But there is another area of foreign policy in which Robertson's beliefs have shaped his positions—his support for General Efrain Rios Montt, a born-again Christian who served briefly as head of the government of Guatemala. At a time when the Reagan administration had cut off aid to Guatemala because of human rights violations, Rios Montt had no stronger supporter than Robertson, who repeatedly defended him. For example, on one program, he called Rios Montt "a great guy" and "impeccably honest." He said Rios Montt is "a very responsible leader. And he's been trying to put down the uprising of communist guerrillas while, at the same time, preserving civil liberties."

Robertson said ("700 Club," March 29, 1983),

We as a people ought to help him; but God wants to help him. So as Christians—forgetting the United States government, we've got a higher power than the United States government—let's appeal to that power to continue to minister in Guatemala. . . . And little by little, that hand is being pacified and the people are being freed from terror and fear. And he [Rios Montt] is putting down wrong-doers and punishing those who are evil-doers. . . . Let it be an example of what God can do when His people are in charge. Lord, it's an alternative to this oligarchy and oppression, and an alternative to Communist terror.

The Amnesty International 1984 report says this about Rios Montt:

During the government of General Efrain Rios Montt (March 1982–August 1983), Amnesty International was also concerned about the promulgation of emergency legislation including a state of siege and Decree 46–82 of July 1982 which established Special Military Tribunals empowered to pass the death penalty for a wide range of political and politically related offenses after summary proceedings, which Amnesty International considered fell far short of international standards for fair trial. Amnesty International was particularly concerned about reports that several of the 15 people executed between September 1982 and March 1983 under its provisions had been convicted solely on the basis of information extracted under torture while held in unacknowledged detention. They had reportedly not been present or legally represented during the proceedings which convicted them.

. . . Amnesty International . . . believed . . . that the Guatemalan military and official civilian defence squads acting under military supervision were responsible for the large-scale extrajudicial execution of non-combatant civilians in the countryside. Amnesty International wrote to the then President Rios Montt on 28 April 1983 calling on the authorities to investigate specific abuses which had allegedly occurred since the Rios Montt administration came to power. These included the reported extrajudicial execution of more than 300 Indian villagers by the Guatemalan army at Agua Fria, Rabinal, Alta Verapaz on 13 September 1982. . . . Although it repeatedly claimed that it was open to investigation from human rights monitoring groups, the Rios Montt administration never replied to Amnesty International's communications, nor did it address the substance of the organization's concerns.

So much for "an example of what God can do when his people are in charge."

For all his condemnations of communism, however, Robertson is quite willing to adopt its methods. He offered these observations on dealing with terrorism in *Christian Life* magazine (August 1986): "I don't think terrorism functions when there is a speedy response to it. The Soviets had four diplomats captured in Lebanon. The KGB took the cousin of one of the terrorists, mutilated his body, delivered it to his relatives and said, 'If our men are not released, the next one is going to get the same treatment.' Now, of course, that is hideously brutal—but the four Soviets were released the next day."

Robertson referred to the US bombing of Libya and said, "If we are going to strike Gadafi we must render him completely and immediately impotent by whatever option we are forced to exercise based on his behavior."

Speaking in California in February 1987, Robertson called for "surgical strikes" and the use of "ferrets" to deal with terrorism—"I frankly would not be against assassination if that were necessary, but it goes against the grain of the American people."

THE LAW ACCORDING TO PAT ROBERTSON

One of Pat Robertson's ancestors signed the Declaration of Independence and, by a strange brand of logic, Robertson believes this makes him an expert on the US Constitution. He spends at least as much time discussing the Constitution as he does any other single issue. But Robertson's views of the Constitution, the federal courts, and the rule of law in general are at odds with the American tradition and represent a major example of the merging of the extremism of his theopolitical views and the extremism of secular right-wing movements; Pat Robertson offers the most sustained attack on the federal judiciary since the John Birch Society and the early days of George Wallace.

Despite his attention to Constitutional issues, Robertson made a remarkable admission in March, 1986, in a speech at his alma mater, Yale Law School. "I must confess," he said, "that when I was at law school . . . I never read the Constitution the whole time I was there."

Robertson added a further confession, telling his audience that he had read the Constitution the weekend before the speech and that "I had never seen it before in my life before I saw it this weekend." When a student asked Robertson how he could be so certain of his interpretation of the Constitution after reading it only once, Robertson backed off, saying he had, in fact, read it before that weekend. But regardless of the date on which Robertson read the Constitution, he clearly failed to understand it.

For example, on December 30, 1982, he declared on the "700 Club," "The Constitution of the United States is a marvelous document for self-government by Christian people. But the minute you turn the document into the hands of non-Christian people and atheist people, they can use it to destroy the very foundations of our society. And that's what's happening."

Robertson has a specific view of the role law should play. On the February 5, 1985, edition of the "700 Club," speaking of the need for strict constructionist judges, he said "The ideal is to change our society . . . the perception and the thinking of the people in our country to come back to a biblical consensus and to understand the Word of God and to meet Jesus Christ." Robertson has said that if he is elected president, he will look for judges who share his judicial philosophy. "I respect the tradition that brought our Constitution into being and the interpretation of it through the early decades of our government."

By the "early decades," he means before 1925, when the Supreme Court ruled that the Bill of Rights applies to state governments as well as the federal government. If the court had not so ruled, the states would have retained the ability to restrict rights to US citizens that the federal government was barred from restricting; they could even establish a state religion. Robertson acknowledges that under his interpretation, the states would be free to establish their own religions, but he argues that they wouldn't because good sense would prevail.

Robertson's most scathing attacks are devoted to the US Supreme Court and, more specifically, to justices who have voted differently than he would; "tyrants," "despots," and "an unelected oligarchy" are his most common descriptions of the court he also refers to as "nine old men in black robes."

Robertson startled those not already familiar with his view of the law in an interview with the editorial board of *The Washington Post* (June 27, 1986). Robertson argued, "A Supreme Court ruling is not the law of the United States. The law of the United States is the Constitution, treaties made in accordance with the Constitution and laws duly enacted by the Congress and signed by the president. And any of these things I would uphold totally with all my strength whether I agreed with them or not."

Robertson claimed that the court's decision in Roe v. Wade, which legalized most abortions, was not the law of the land because it was based on "very faulty law." He added that as a private citizen, "I am bound by the laws of the United States and all fifty states . . . [but] I am not bound by any case or any court to which I am not a party. . . . I don't think the Congress is subservient to the courts. . . . They can ignore a Supreme Court ruling if they so choose."

The *Post* interview did not mark the first time that Robertson had offered this view. For example, on the April 29, 1982, "700 Club" he said,

One thing that you might not be aware of is what the Supreme Court says is not, in American history, the law of the land. A court merely decides a dispute of two parties before it, but only can an elected legislature with the concurrence of the executive, also elected, put a law into effect. The Supreme Court has claimed in a recent decision, in the last twenty years, that what it says is the 'supreme law of the land'— but it is not. It does not have and should not have under our constitutional system the force of law put into effect by elected representatives. And this is something we need to understand because we are now coming to the point where legislation is being made by judges who hold office for life. And that, ladies and gentlemen, is wrong.

On October 23, 1987, on the "700 Club," Robertson said "Supreme Court decisions are binding in the court systems and are evidence. . . . But in terms of general law which binds every citizen— why should you and I be bound because of the ineptitude, if you will, or the skill of one or more defense lawyers, or the plaintiffs in any particular lawsuit?"

Robertson's views amount to nothing less than an endorsement of anarchy. What Robertson says, in effect, is that neither private individuals, presidents, nor members of Congress are bound to obey or enforce laws with which they disagree. If that is the case, the role of law disappears. As president, Robertson would be free, for example, to work to reverse Roe v. Wade, but he would not have the option of not enforcing it.

The *Philadelphia Inquirer* reacted to Robertson's views this way: "His denial of judicial authority constitutes nothing less than denial of the Constitution in theory and practice. Therefore, he disqualifies himself from eligibility to be president, for he could not truthfully abide by the oath requiring him to 'preserve, protect and defend the Constitution of the United States.' "

Robertson's cavalier attitude toward the Constitution was reflected in his defense of the appointment of Daniel Manion to a federal judgeship. He complained that at Manion's confirmation hearing, senators had badgered him by asking if he would accept Supreme Court decisions with which he disagreed. Robertson said, "Well, you shouldn't ask a judicial candidate whether or not he will go along with every, every bad decision of all the courts that preceded him."

Robertson has also endorsed one strategy to change court rulings that has already been soundly and widely rejected—the kind of court-packing that Franklin Roosevelt unsuccessfully attempted:

All that is needed today to change it [the size of the Supreme Court] is a simply majority of the Congress and a sign into law by the President. And we would suddenly have 11 Supreme Court justices instead of 9 and possibly with a 6–5 majority of people who cared for the original intent of the Framers, we could change the whole thing! It's that simple. And I might also add that they do not serve for life, they serve for good behavior. There are many people who feel this is no longer good behavior. They have sworn to uphold the Constitution, not rewrite it and destroy it as they have so cynically set out to do ("700 Club," May 1, 1986).

Robertson's aversion to the federal judiciary is not new. In 1981, he outlined a five-point plan to regulate federal court power: 1) create national dialogue leading to court self-restraint; 2) regulate the appointment process from Capitol Hill; 3) limit appellate jurisdiction of federal courts; 4) abolish the lower federal courts; and 5) pass a constitutional amendment limiting court power.

Robertson's concern with changing the court system is so strong that he has virtually admitted that his support for a constitutional amendment to restore organized vocal prayer to the classroom is simply part of his plan for the federal courts. According to the *Baptist Press,* June 7, 1986, he told the Religion Newswriters Association, "School prayer is sort of a code word. It doesn't mean anything really. I think it would be a step in the right direction possibly. What matters is a return to basic discipline and morality and getting power to the people."

Robertson's attempt to undermine the federal judiciary rejects the constitutional separation of powers among the executive, legislative, and judicial branches. Robertson said at Yale that he had discovered that the Constitution devoted 255 lines to the legislative branch, 114 to the chief executive, and 44 to the federal courts. From this simple accounting, he concluded that the Founding Fathers didn't want a separation of powers after all, that Congress is "where our founders intended the seat of power in Washington to be."

Ironically, Robertson's attack on the separation of powers strikes at one key element of the Constitution which was clearly shaped by religious belief—the widespread belief in the concept of original sin; the founders, aware of the human tendency toward corruption, wanted to prevent any one branch of government from usurping power in a tyrannical way.

They were particularly concerned that the majority, working through Congress, should not violate the rights of the minority; that's why they gave the courts the power to defend those rights. Similarly, giving Congress and the states the ability to amend the Constitution places important checks on the judiciary. To place, in effect, absolute power in the hands of Congress, as Robertson would do, is to invite precisely the kind of abuse of power that the founders designed the Constitution to prevent.

Robertson has added one final twist to his constitutional theory: if all else fails, let God do it. In a speech to the National Right to Life Committee in Denver, he said abortion opponents could look to "the wonderful process of the mortality tables" to change the make-up of the court and bring about a new decision on abortion. Robertson later escalated his "pray-for-death" rhetoric, telling abortion opponents "to pray somehow that those gentlemen on the Supreme Court, a couple of them, will either take retirement or be graduated to that great courtroom in the sky" (*St. Louis Post-Dispatch,* March 13, 1987).

This was not the first time Robertson had used the rhetoric of violence in relation to the courts. On November 15, 1981, he complained to his "700 Club" audience about an ACLU lawsuit attempting to bar the city of Providence, Rhode Island, from displaying a nativity scene. Robertson said, "I'm not one who advocates revolution, but so help me, if they keep it up we ought to revolt. I mean, this is an unelected tyranny."

Pat Robertson's views on the American legal system are not the views of a conservative who merely differs on key matters of judicial interpretation; they are the views of a radical who wants to debilitate the courts as a barrier to the exercise of the brute force of a majority scornful about the rights of the minority.

EDUCATION

Pat Robertson is not satisfied with attempting to remake the American judicial system; he is also taking aim at the public school system. On the "700 Club," October 5, 1981, he said, "There are two major elites who are working in conjunction to take away the religious heritage from our nation. . . . The first is the educational elite. . . . In league with them are many people in the judicial system, the legal system."

Robertson told "700 Club" viewers on November 24, 1982, that America's public schools are more dangerous than "any place else." Why? Because "the public schools are actually agencies for the promotion of another religion, which is the humanist religion" (October 2, 1981).

Robertson has likened US public schools to Nazi and Communist indoctrination centers: "The state steadily is attempting to do something that a few states other than the Nazis and the Soviets have attempted to do, namely, to take the children away from the parents and to educate them in a philosophy that is amoral, anti-Christian, and humanistic and to show them a collectivistic philosophy that will ultimately lead toward Marxism, socialism and a communistic type of ideology" ("700 Club," May 13, 1984).

Robertson is not satisfied with linking the public schools to Nazism and communism. In *Answers,* he says, "The humanism that is being taught in our schools, media and intellectual circles will ultimately lead people to the Antichrist, because he will be the consummate figure of humanism."

For Robertson, the solution is simply: get government out of the schools:

Ladies and gentlemen, the tragic thing is that education has failed. Now, there are many dedicated teachers, there are many dedicated educators and educational administrators. But on the whole, so-called progressive education, which has at its roots a moralless society or a society without moral instruction, and the current pedagogy is a dismal, horrible failure and the only answer is for parents to take back the education of our children" ("700 Club," April 21, 1986).

"The ultimate solution," Robertson has said, "is that we have to work to get the state out of the business of educating kids at the primary and secondary levels, and get that education back in the hands of the parents where it belongs" ("700 Club," October 2, 1981).

Robertson developed creative ways to undermine public schools. He told the *Atlanta Constitution* on April 4, 1987, that "if elected, he would cut off federal education aid to school systems where SAT scores were on the decline and illiteracy was on the rise."

One target of Robertson's attack on public education is the National Education Association (NEA). In an attack on the NEA on the "700 Club," November 20, 1984, he said, "The teachers who are teaching your children . . . are not necessarily nice, wonderful servants of the community. They are activists supporting one party and one set of values and a number of the values which they espouse are: affirmative action, ERA, gun control legislation, sex education, illegal teachers' strikes, nuclear freeze, federal funding for abortions, decriminalization of marijuana, etc."

Robertson's hatred of public education extends to education programs for very young children, including Headstart, one of the most successful federal education programs of all time, Robertson opposes

Headstart because "if you're smart you'll catch up anyway" ("700 Club," March 28, 1984).

As long as there are public schools, Robertson believes, they should teach Creationism, the Fundamentalist alternative to evolution. Robertson also charges that American textbook publishers are part of a plot against religion—"We're talking about a deliberate expunging of a major portion of the history of this nation in order to get this nation on a different course than the one it's had for the last two hundred to three hundred years" ("700 Club," April 1, 1986).

In recent years, Robertson has adopted a new tactic in his attack on public education. His National Legal Foundation supported parents in Mobile, Alabama, who charged that the Mobile school district violated their religious freedom by teaching "the religion of secular humanism." The parents charged that the absence of Christian beliefs in textbooks amounted to advocacy of secular humanism. Federal Judge Brevard Hand ruled in favor of the parents and barred some forty textbooks from the Mobile schools. People for the American Way joined the legal fight on the side of the school board, and Judge Hand's decision was overturned by a federal appeals court in August 1987.

Robertson is also opposed to any state regulation of Christian schools. In criticizing a Texas effort to include church-run schools under the state education code, ("700 Club," April 10, 1986) he said,

There does seem to be an attempt to grab power and a very powerful union to take more and more control. . . . And these private schools are a threat to them. You see, they represent free enterprise, and we believe in free enterprise and the American way, which is challenge and competition. But when you have a monopoly, you have no challenge and no competition. . . . If you don't get diligent, you will find that you've lost a number of your liberties.

To Pat Robertson, education seems to be indoctrination in Fundamentalist tenets, more than it is anything else.

WOMEN'S RIGHTS AND FAMILY LIFE

When it comes to the family, Robertson is not simply old-fashioned; he exhibits a "blame-the-victim" mentality which blames divorce, juvenile delinquency, homosexuality, sex changes, and a variety of social ills on the fact that so many women today do not accept the biblical ideal of submission to their husbands.

Robertson summarizes his beliefs about marriage and family life in *Answers:*

The apostle Paul, writing to the church of Ephesus, laid down some very good guidelines for husbands and wives. To the men, he said "Husbands, love your wives, just as Christ also loved the Church and gave himself for it." To the women, he said "Wives, submit to your own husbands, as to the Lord." That kind of relationship brings about a lack of tension in marriage.

The one who always insists on rights will destroy the marriage relationship. If the husband says to his wife, "You must obey me because the Bible says so," he is going to alienate her. At the same time, the wife who refuses to submit to the husband and fights him all the time will make him apprehensive about following the Lord: He will start thinking, "What if I get a message from God? All I am going to get is opposition from my wife, so I might as well just follow my own desires and let her follow hers." Such attitudes will pull couples apart, whereas God's standards should draw them together.

Robertson has frequently elaborated on this view on television. For example, on the "700 Club," December 10, 1982, he offered this advice to women trying to convert their husbands: "Please don't make your husbands think that in order to accept Jesus Christ, they have to submit to you, because no macho man wants to do that. They'll submit to Jesus, but they kind of like to be the head of the household. And that's scriptural. And that's the way it should be."

Robertson also had this advice for a woman who said her husband wanted her to go to work ("700 Club," January 28, 1983):

A wife gives tremendous ability to a husband, no question about it. Instead of being able to earn $17,000, maybe he can earn $30,000 or $40,000 a year; because his mind can be free to concentrate on the business. So, husbands, if you've got any sense, you've got a good thing going for you; you don't know how fortunate you are. Don't try to send your wife out to work and push her out. Say: "Help me." And then you begin to look to God to let you excel, because you have the secret weapon that us husbands better appreciate.

But while wives may be a "secret weapon," Robertson is quick to assign them blame:

Unless the mothers, especially in our society, are willing to give up the so-called immediate quest for self-identity, and are willing to submerge themselves, if you will, into the good of the family unit, and ultimately, the good of all society, we're going to have terrible problems, as we're having young people grow up without love. We have teenage delinquents and juvenile delinquents. We have people who themselves are not willing to form a lasting relationship in marriage, because they haven't had role models in the past. We have people with changing sex identities, women who want to be men, and men who want to be women, so they form homosexual relationships. There is this tearing apart of the family and it's not going to end until people are saying "I will give myself to God Almighty. I will submit to his will" ("700 Club," January 18, 1983).

Robertson returns to this theme again and again:

Why are so many marriages falling apart? Why is the divorce rate so high? . . . Why is there such tragedy in marriage? Why do we here at CBN have 700,000 calls last year dealing with family and marriage problems? Well, the reason is selfishness. . . . Now the basic answer to the basic problem of marriages today is a question of surrender. We don't like to surrender and we don't like to serve. . . . There is a question of headship. The wife actually makes the husband the head of the household and she looks to him and she says "Now you pray, and I'm going to pray for you that the Lord will speak to you" ("700 Club," May 22, 1986).

In Pat Robertson's world, God apparently doesn't speak to women.

A PAT ROBERTSON SAMPLER

On AIDS

"We have a bankruptcy of morality and AIDS is the consequence" ("700 Club," May 2, 1986).

On Civil Rights

The Civil Rights Restoration Act (designed to overturn the Supreme Court's Grove City College ruling which loosened civil rights standards in private colleges) is "one of the most frightening pieces of legislation that has been brought up" ("700 Club," February 25, 1985).

On the Equal Rights Amendment

In criticizing the ERA, Robertson noted that the amendment did not mention men or women, but only referred to sex. "What people are not sure of, and this is—I'm not being facetious—they're not sure of whether it would be interpreted, your gender, or how you perform sex" ("700 Club," February 23, 1982).

On the Federal Reserve Board

"Now, at the present time, the president is elected by the people. His economic policies are one thing and here's an unelected man [the Federal Reserve chairman] in charge of a quasi-private organization who is just as powerful. A president can put us on the road to prosperity and this unelected man can put us into a depression, merely by regulating the money supply. It's a very, very dangerous thing for people who love democracy and I think more and more there's a groundswell beginning to build in this country that says in matters dealing with the vital interest of all of us, the people have to be in control of what's being done" ("700 Club," June 11, 1986).

On Government Social Programs

Speaking on the "700 Club" on October 4, 1984, Robertson said, "In the last few years . . . the Evangelical Christians have withdrawn from the arena and given over the job of education . . . [and] feeding the poor and needy. . . . They've given those things over to the government, and now the liberal churches cry for more federal intervention. . . . The NCC [National Council of Churches] . . . who would be considered theologically liberal are wanting more government intervention. And it's impossible to say take the government away from our churches, which is what most Christian people want, and at the same time say we must let the government take care of the mentally handicapped, of those who are poor and needy. . . . We can't give all of that plus the moral order of the family and the protection of battered wives and children . . . to the state and expect the state to stay our of our lives."

On Halloween

"I think we ought to close Halloween down. . . . Do you want your children to dress up like witches? . . . The Druids used to dress up like this when they were doing human sacrifice. . . . They [your children] are acting out Satanic rituals and participating in it, and don't even realize it" ("700 Club," October 29, 1982).

On the Nuclear Freeze Movement

"The nuclear freeze movement in the United States is carefully being orchestrated from Europe by people who are clearly allied to either Socialist causes, or, more than Socialist, Communist-Soviet causes. . . . There are well-meaning people in the nuclear freeze movement, but there is also no question that the Soviets are behind it, orchestrating it carefully in Europe and here, according to testimonies" ("700 Club," October 7, 1982).

On Social Security

"There's one way out of the Social Security system . . . I really believe, and that is to turn the thing over to private industry" ("700 Club," May 28, 1982).

"Senator Helms said: 'What we really ought to do is to make Social Security private.' And I couldn't agree with him more" ("700 Club," March 10, 1983).

On Urban Aid

Robertson has a novel way to undermine urban aid. He has proposed "replacing most federal urban aid programs with a system of voluntary contributions supported by a 10 percent income tax credit." (*Washington Post*, June 17, 1987).

Legal Services

Robertson says the Legal Services Corporation "promoted 250,000 divorces. . . . Almost a quarter of all divorces in America were the responsibility of that one agency" (Jackson, Michigan, *Citizen-Patriot*, March 22, 1987).

Jews and Heaven

Robertson told Phil Donahue on September 29, 1986 that Jews can get into Heaven by practicing animal sacrifice:

"Jews go to Heaven in relation to their own religion. And what does their religion say? It's very clear, they go to Heaven if they keep all the commandments of the Jewish law, and if you go back into the Old Testament, you see that it was necessary in case they didn't to have animal sacrifice. That's what was set up in the Old Testament. And in accordance with keeping all of their law, they are God's chosen people, there's no question about it.

" . . . Now the Jews have a little different deal. If they want to keep their law, if they want to fulfill the covenant, if they want to have sacrifices provided for in the Book of Leviticus, then that is what's available for them. That's the way it is."

The Iran-Contra Scandal

Robertson's disregard for the Constitution is reflected in his lack of concern about the moral implications and constitutional threat present in the Iran-Contra scandal. In fact, Robertson sees no scandal in the behavior of administration officials who ignored the Constitution in pursuing secret policies. "The United States Congress and the press, the major newspapers don't want to do anything to free a country in the western hemisphere from communist domination. That is the scandal" (Concord, New Hampshire, *Monitor*, May 27, 1987).

CONCLUSION

When one takes the time to examine Pat Robertson's worldview in his own words, it becomes clear that he is an extremist. He claims to work miracles and identifies himself with God and those who disagree with him with Satan—or with ideologies he says are Satanic, like atheism, communism, or "secular humanism."

Robertson cites a divine mandate for specific political objectives from his reading of the Bible and from his personal conversations with God. He would obliterate the separation of church and state and the separation of powers; he would dismantle the federal courts, the public schools, the Social Security system, the Federal Reserve Board, and government social programs, leaving the federal government with nothing to do except advocate sectarian beliefs, fight Communists, and guarantee the government securities that God told him to buy.

Pat Robertson is not just another conservative; he's an extremist with a baby face.

7. Catholics and the Seamless Garment

"Personally Opposed, but . . ."

In a major speech on the eve of the 1984 elections, Joseph Cardinal Bernardin of Chicago noted,

Elections are wonderful and necessary events in the democratic process. However, they are not well suited for producing reflective ideas or careful distinctions. The questions which have run through this election—about the role of religion in our public life, the relation of political responses to moral issues—are broader and deeper than election politics can handle. I recommend that we use the experiences of the moment to help set the agenda for the future.

Bernardin and other leading bishops have addressed religion and politics questions regularly since 1984. The internal Catholic debate on mixing religion and politics deserves close study for several reasons: it is the most sustained, high-level debate on the subject now being conducted in American religious circles; if the bishops develop sound principles, they can be of use to other denominations. Finally, the Catholic church in the United States has a tenuous relationship with the Religious Right: on the hand, they agree on issues such as abortion and tuition tax credits; on the other hand, they disagree on just about everything else, including arms control, Central America, South Africa, and the economy.

THE STATE OF THE DEBATE

The starting point for examining the bishops' contribution to the religion and politics debate is the statement on "Political Responsibility in an Election Year" issued March 22, 1984, by the US Catholic Conference Administrative Board. The statement, updated from 1979, said,

The Church's role in the political order includes the following:

- Education regarding the teachings of the church and the responsibilities of the faithful.
- Analysis of issues for their social and moral dimension.
- Measuring public policy against gospel values.
- Participating with other concerned parties in debate over public policy.
- Speaking out with courage, skill and concern on public issues involving human rights, social justice, and the life of the church in society.

Unfortunately, our efforts in this area are sometimes misunderstood. The church's participation in public affairs is not a threat to the political process or to genuine pluralism, but an affirmation of their importance. The church recognizes the legitimate autonomy of government and the right of all, including the church itself, to be heard in the formulation of public policy.

We specifically do not seek the formation of a religious voting bloc. Nor do we wish to instruct people on how they should vote by endorsing candidates. We urge citizens to avoid choosing candidates simply on the basis of personal self-interest. Rather, we hope that voters will examine the positions of candidates on the full range of issues, as well as their integrity, philosophy and performance.

The political responsibility statement listed a number of issues of concern, including abortion, arms control, opposition to capital punishment, support for civil rights, education programs, national health insurance, and an emphasis on human rights in foreign policy. While the bishops are consistently seen as supporting the Republicans because of their support for a constitutional amendment on abortion and tuition tax credit legislation, on virtually every other issue they are far closer to the Democratic platform.

The bishops added further to the religion-and-politics debate with their pastoral letter, "Economic Justice for All: Catholic Social Teaching and the US Economy," issued in November 1986. Like the 1983 pastoral, "The Challenge of Peace," the new document received the most attention for its approach to issues and policy recommendations. But both pastorals also make important distinctions about church pronouncements in the political arena. In "The Challenge of Peace," for example, the bishops pointed out that "not every statement in this letter has the same moral authority." In some cases, the bishops said, they were stating universal moral principles—such as the prohibition against the direct taking of innocent life. In other cases, however, they said "prudential judgments are involved based on specific circumstances which can change or which can be interpreted differently by people of good will." The bishops gave an example: while they were convinced that support for a US pledge never to be the first to use nuclear weapons was a good idea, they said, it was not a position which was binding on the conscience of Catholics.

In "Economic Justice for All," the bishops again made clear that they were talking to two audiences: "We write, then, first of all to provide guidance for members of our own church as they seek to form their consciences about economic matters. . . . At the same time, we want to add our voice to the public debate about the directions in which the US economy should be moving. We seek the cooperation and support of those who do not share our faith or tradition."

The bishops' peace and economic pastorals have created an interesting double standard: liberal Democrats who criticize the bishops' handling of the abortion issue welcome and praise their statements supporting arms control and government social programs, while their staunchest supporters on abortion go out of their way to discredit the bishops' liberal positions on other issues.

The first bishop to address the mixing of religion and politics after the 1984 elections was Bishop James Malone of Youngstown, Ohio, in his presidential address at the bishops' November 1984 general meeting less than a week after the elections. Malone said that the church had a responsibility to help shape public opinion. "I believe it is precisely the role of the church in shaping public opinion which deserves more specific attention," he said. "The relationship of the church to public opinion locates our distinctive role theologically and constitutionally in a democracy. . . . It is hardly ever possible to translate public opinion directly into a policy position. But public opinion does set an atmosphere and a framework within which decisions are made by elected and appointed officials."

But, Malone said, "In the public arena of a pluralistic democracy, leaders face the same tests of rational argument as any other individuals or institutions. Our impact on the public will be directly proportionate to the persuasiveness of our positions. We seek no special status and we should not be accorded one."

Malone repeated his rejection of a single-issue approach to politics: "The inner logic of Catholic moral principles has taught us to join issues rather than to isolate them. We oppose a 'single-issue' strategy because only by addressing a broad spectrum of issues can we do justice to the moral tradition we possess as a Church and thereby demonstrate the moral challenges we face as a nation."

Malone's comments represented a highroad expression of a basic fact of life in American politics. Any group that sells its support to one political party on the basis of a single issue loses its influence with everyone. If the Republicans believe they have the bishops in their pocket on the basis of abortion, they don't have to pay any attention to them on other issues, particularly where they disagree. And if the Democrats believe the bishops are in the Republicans' pocket, they don't have to pay attention to them at all. One example makes the point well: the late Terence Cardinal Cooke of New York was chairman of the bishops Ad Hoc Committee on Pro-Life Activities, but he was at equally home in Jimmy Carter's and Ronald Reagan's White House; it's impossible to imagine Cardinal O'Connor getting a friendly reception from a Democratic president.

Malone returned to the religion-and-politics issue in a major speech at the University of Notre Dame in early 1986. He repeated the distinction made in the pastoral letters between the levels of authority with which the bishops speak. "It is entirely within the church's competence," he said, "to teach authoritatively that direct abortion and direct attacks on noncombatants in war are incompatible with that respect for life which ought to be a controlling principle of individual and social behavior."

At the same time, he said, the church does not speak with the same degree of authority when it talks about specific public policy proposals. "As to what should be done," he said, "the institutional church can offer suggestions, give encouragement and support, alone or in coalition with others engaged in advocacy on behalf of politics and programs which give promise of achieving the desired results.

"But it must in the final analysis respect the right of Catholic citizens, candidates and officeholders, acting with informed consciences and in the light of prudence, to discern and advocate other practical measures of achieving the same results."

This was the strongest affirmation by a leading bishop to date of the right to conscience in the political arena; the political responsibility statement and others had alluded to it in a much less direct manner. While recognizing Catholics' right of conscience, Malone also said,

Sincerity minimally requires that those who say they stand with the church's teaching but reject the bishops' policy proposals offer genuine alternatives calculated to realize the same purposes.

If some see the bishops' goal of a Constitutional amendment to restore legal protection to the unborn as unachievable, what will they do instead to bring about legal protection? If some reject the bishops' advocacy of human rights criteria in US foreign policy, what specific measures do they support for fostering and protecting human rights in allies and client nations of the United States?

Malone's speech clearly accepted the Cuomo position of respectful political dissent, but perhaps only up to a point. To the bishops, "legal protection" means making abortion illegal, and it gives very little ground to insist that a candidate opposed to making abortion illegal through one route must do so through another.

Cardinal Bernardin returned several times to the development of the "consistent ethic of life," or "seamless garment," argument. He continued to draw heavily on the thought of John Courtney Murray, the late Jesuit theologian who was an expert on church-state matters and whose work led to the Second Vatican Council's adoption of a statement on religious liberty. Bernardin delivered a particularly important speech at the University of Portland in Oregon in October 1986. He discussed five major issues in the debate:

- Civil discourse in the United States is influenced, widely shaped, by religious pluralism. . . . The genius of American pluralism, in his [Murray's] view, was that it provided for the religious freedom of each citizen and every faith. However, it did not purchase tolerance at the price of expelling religious and moral values from the public life of the nation.

- There is a legitimate secularity of the political process, just as there is a legitimate role for religious and moral discourse in our nation's life. . . . Today's religious institutions, I believe, must reaffirm their rights and recognize their limits. . . . The limits relate not to whether we enter the public debate, but how we advocate a public case. This implies, for example, that religiously rooted positions somehow must be translated into language, arguments and categories which a religiously pluralistic society can agree on as the moral foundation of key policy positions.

- All participants in the discourse must face the test of complexity. . . . We owe the public a careful accounting of how we have come to our moral conclusions.

- We must keep in mind the relationship between civil law and morality. Although the premises of civil law are rooted in moral principles, the scope of law is more limited and its purpose is not the moralization of society. . . . [I]t is not the function of civil law to enjoin or prohibit everything that moral principles enjoin or prohibit. History has shown over and over again that people cherish freedom; they can be coerced only minimally. When we pursue a course of legal action, therefore, we must ask whether the requirements of public order are serious enough to take precedence over the claims of freedom.

- How do we determine which issues are public moral questions and which are best defined as private moral questions? For Murray, an issue was one of public morality if it affected the public order of society. Public order in turn encompassed three goods: public peace, essential protection of human rights, and commonly accepted standards of moral behavior in a community. . . . Today we have a public consensus in law and policy which clearly defines civil rights as issues of public morality and the decision to drink alcoholic beverages as clearly one of private morality. But neither decision was reached without struggle. The consensus was not automatic on either equation. Philosophers, activists, politicians, preachers, judges and ordinary citizens had to state a case, shape a consensus and then find a way to give the consensus public standing in the life of the nation.

Finally, Bernardin outlined a list of questions which he said remain to be addressed:

What role does consensus play in the development of public policy and civil law? Earlier I suggested that its role is essential in the long run. But what about the short term? Moreover, what are the appropriate roles of civic and religious leaders in providing moral leadership in the public policy debate within a pluralistic community? What is the difference between a bishop's role and a politician's in the public debate about moral issues which the consistent ethic embraces? Should a politician wait until a consensus is developed before taking a stand or initiating legislation?

Must a Catholic office seeker or officeholder work for all clearly identified Catholic concerns simultaneously and with the same vigor? Is that possible? If such a person need not work for all these concerns aggressively and at the same time, on what basis does one decide what to concentrate on and what not? Does theology provide the answer, or politics, or both? What guidelines does one use to determine which issues are so central to Catholic belief that they must be pursued legislatively regardless of the practical consequences of passage? What are the consequences if a Catholic office seeker or officeholder does not follow the church's teaching in the campaign for or exercise of public office?

What is a Catholic officeholder's responsibility, in light of the Second Vatican Council's *Declaration on Religious Liberty,* to protect the religious beliefs of non-Catholics? What is his or her responsibility under the Constitution? How are these responsibilities related?

How is the distinction between accepting a moral principle and making prudential judgments about applying it in particular circumstances—for example, in regard to specific legislation— worked out in the political order? What is the responsibility of a Catholic officeholder or office seeker when the bishops have made a prudential judgment regarding specific legislation? How are Catholic voters to evaluate a Catholic officeholder or office seeker who accepts a moral principle, and not only disagrees with the bishops regarding specific legislation, but supports its defeat?

Another voice in the Catholic discussion of religion and politics was Archbishop Rembert Weakland of Milwaukee, who chaired the committee which drafted the bishops' economic pastoral. He addressed the relationship of church to government in a talk to the Wisconsin state assembly on February 5, 1987. Weakland distinguished the roles of politicians and religious leaders:

Politics, by its nature, must be the art of the possible. With limited resources and with so many points of view and interests to be reconciled, politicians must often find ways of satisfying all concerned and balance many conflicting currents. Religious leaders can be more prophetic, more demanding, less compromising, less flexible. Their duty to society is to keep the moral principles clear in the midst of the concrete imperfect realization of a moral ideal.

No religion should become a political party nor align itself with only one. I can say clearly and without hesitation that the Catholic church in our country will not align itself with any particular party. Such an alignment would be bad for politics, but worse for religion. Thus it should not surprise you if the Catholic church seems to be politically ambivalent, aligning itself nationally with the conservative and right wing of the Republican Party on issues such as abortion and with the more liberal Democrats on many social issues, capital punishment, and the rights of labor. At times this can be confusing, and I always smile when people assume that, since a religious leader accepts one aspect of a party platform, he or she accepts a whole series of issues connected with that platform.

Weakland also spoke of the right of conscience:

We certainly would not want all Catholics to feel . . . that the positions they take or the options they voice must be the official positions or opinions of their church. Yet we know that some issues will be much more central to their church's teaching and thus less open to compromise and debate. We wrestle with the need of the politician to be true to that faith commitment and yet free to work out pragmatic solutions that are realistic in any given situation. We do not have absolute clarity on those points yet.

The Catholic church is still struggling with how it should relate to constitutional governments. Its history in this area outside the United States has been mostly a post–World War II phenomenon—a period relatively short in the long history of the Roman Catholic church. Here in the United States, the Catholic church has enjoyed great freedom, but only after the period of John F. Kennedy has it begun to enter more fully into the national debate on social and political issues. Before that, it spoke mostly to its own constituency and on very specific political issues where Catholics had a direct involvement.

Referring to the relationship of law and morality, he said, "We can never ask that all law under such a constitutional government mirror Catholic morality; but we do see that law also has its own didactic force in the morality of a society. We know that under such a constitutional arrangement we must do more to alert our people that not everything permitted by law is morally acceptable to Catholic standards. We have been negligent in this regard."

Cardinal O'Connor of New York addressed the religion-and-politics issue in a June 1986 speech to the Catholic Press Association. He asked how the church should move from the theoretical to the practical when dealing with moral issues in the public arena, and conceded, "I don't pretend to know the answer to this key question. Indeed, as one who has blundered more frequently than most in attempting the transition from concern to action, I have demonstrated rather dramatically that I don't know the answer."

But O'Connor complained that Catholic church involvement in politics was limited by "Catholic self-consciousness." He rejected church endorsement of candidates, but said "that we alone, the 'Roman' church, with all the sinister overtones that title conveys, should have to be excruciatingly meticulous about every word spoken, every step taken— this without question imposes on us extraordinary restrictions as we attempt to affect public policy."

O'Connor avoided major gaffes during the 1986 elections, in which Cuomo was reelected as governor by a landslide. He did, however, bar Catholic politicians who disagreed with church positions from speaking about political issues in New York archdiocesan parishes. This move, if implemented to the letter, would exclude virtually all Catholic politicians; but in context it was obviously aimed at those who disagreed with the church on abortion.

In early 1987, O'Connor led a major delegation of priests, nuns, and laity involved with the New York Catholic Conference in a lobbying visit to the state legislature in Albany; the group urged legislators to support the church's position on a wide variety of issues, from abortion to welfare reform, from parochial school aid to aid for the homeless. O'Connor claimed to be speaking for 6.6 million Catholics in the state. At one point, he said, "Neither the Governor nor anyone else, as the Governor so well knows, has the right to violate the Bible or moral law on the grounds that this will achieve some good for the people here and now."

CRITIQUE OF THE DEBATE

Cardinal Bernardin, Bishop Malone, Archbishop Weakland, and others have made an important contribution to the debate on the mixing of religion and politics in America. Much of what they set out could and should be used as a model by other religious groups. But their position is not without flaws and unanswered questions.

First, the positive contributions, which can be summarized this way:

- Religious leaders speak to two audiences, their members and the society at large, and must speak in language appropriate to each.
- Religious leaders speak with the authority of their office when they teach church doctrine and broad moral principles to their members; but when they address specific public policy choices, they do not speak with that level of authority.
- Religious leaders have a responsibility to teach their members that civil law is not designed to bar everything the church considers immoral and that, at the same time, not everything that is legal is moral.
- Religious leaders have a right to speak out on public issues without either being restricted or receiving special treatment.
- When religious leaders do speak out on public issues, they must do so in a way that appeals to social morality, not church doctrine, and is persuasive to those of different faiths.

- Religious leaders should be non-partisan.
- Religious leaders should reject a single-issue approach.
- Religious leaders must respect the right of citizens, candidates, and public officials to disagree in good conscience.

While this may represent a consensus among the bishops' leadership and the views of a solid majority of bishops, it does not have unanimous support. Some still hold to a single-issue approach which views abortion as the most critical and ultimately decisive issue in determining how to vote. Others simply practice a double standard: they refuse to treat abortion the same way they treat arms control, economics, and other issues. On those other issues, they take pains to point out that people of good will differ on prudential judgments on political issues and to emphasize that when they recommend specific public policy positions, they do not speak with the same degree of authority as they do on general principles. The bishops would be far better received in the public debate if they simply acknowledged that the same criteria apply to abortion. An added problem is that bishops who hold a single-issue approach have no qualms about appearing to endorse Republicans, while bishops who back the "seamless garment" approach go out of their way to avoid appearing favorable toward a Democratic who is pro-choice.

But other problems remain as well. Archbishop Weakland identified a key difficulty when he said the Catholic church is still learning how to function in a constitutional democracy. The American bishops are learning how to speak as church to the public debate; but they are still wrestling with how to speak to Catholic public officials within a pluralistic society. Cardinal O'Connor argues that a Catholic public official has no right to deny "the Bible or moral law." Even Cardinal Bernardin's questions imply that Catholic public officials have a special obligation to their church as they perform their duties; questions about a Catholic legislator's responsibilities under the constitution have come far later than they should have in the bishops' debate. The bishops seem to be particularly confused about just who Catholic bishops and Catholic public officials represent.

O'Connor argues that the bishops are too sensitive to concern about the "Roman" church speaking out on public issues. But

Americans have become more—not less—sensitized to Vatican efforts to influence politics in the wake of actions by the Vatican itself: In early 1987, for example, Pope John Paul II visited Argentina and opposed efforts to legalize divorce there; just a few months earlier, Joseph Cardinal Ratzinger, head of the Vatican Congregation for the Doctrine of the Faith, issued a statement on biomedical issues, which demanded that civil law bar the use of new birth-related technologies, from *in vitro* fertilization to surrogate motherhood. Catholic leaders cannot afford to be insensitive to the fact that it is an article of faith to Americans that no outside power—no church, no government, no union leader—dictate how any American votes.

It's clear, then, that Cardinal O'Connor was wrong when, in lobbying the New York legislature, he said he was speaking *for* 6.6 million Catholics in the state. He could certainly claim that when it comes to the church's positions, he speaks *to* 6.6 million New York Catholics. But when it comes to public policy matters, he cannot speak for anyone but himself and the New York Catholic Conference, the civil agency formed by the church to influence public policy. He and the other bishops have a right to do that, of course, but they do not represent the state's Catholics because they were not elected to do so. They may urge the state's Catholics—who hold a variety of positions on all issues—to contact their legislators on particular issues. If New York Catholics do choose to urge their legislators to take a particular course of action, they are simply exercising their rights as citizens, with no special voice because they are Catholics. They also speak out with the recognition that, just as some of their representatives are Democrats and some are Republicans, some of their representatives are Catholics, some are Protestants, and some are Jews.

Public officials represent their constituencies and their consciences. A Catholic governor or congressman does not represent the Catholic church anymore than a Methodist governor or congressman represents the Methodist church. Catholic public officials may have an obligation as Catholics to use church teaching to form their own consciences; but when it comes to acting, they must rely on their conscience and their commitment to uphold the Constitution, not on church teaching.

The bishops are frustrated when a Catholic politician like Geraldine Ferarro says, "I'm personally opposed to abortion, but I don't want to impose my religious views on others." The bishops argue that if a politician believes an act is immoral, he or she must act against it.

In this exchange, both parties are wrong. Abortion is, by its very nature, both a public and private issue. Even if the final decision is to keep abortion legal, the process of debate is itself public. There are also a number of public policy questions related to abortion: government funding, regulations, the rights of minors, programs to help women with problem pregnancies, government policies which encourage or discourage abortion. Portraying abortion as a strictly doctrinal or a private issue without public implications does a disservice to public debate.

But in arguing that a Catholic politician who is morally opposed to abortion must support a constitutional amendment to limit it, the bishops ignore the distinction between moral and civil law. They also ignore the claim that religious leaders must argue issues on their merits. A Catholic legislator, like any other, may be convinced that there are moral, civil religion grounds on which to outlaw abortion; but if the same legislator wants to outlaw abortion simply *because* his church tells him to, he would be violating the spirit of the Constitution. And if the same legislator believes that abortion should remain legal, the church must respect his or her conscience as a legislator.

On a practical level, Americans understand that their officials have personal interests; they expect that a black representative will pay some additional attention to issues affecting blacks; they expect that a Jewish representative will devote extra time to issues affecting peace in the Middle East; they expect that an Irish Catholic senator will be concerned about the situation in Northern Ireland. But Americans also expect that these areas of special interest will not interfere with their representatives' ability to represent *all* the people.

In short, when the bishops exercise their own constitutional right to speak out on public issues, they must, as Bernardin and Malone argue, rely on their ability to persuade public officials on the basis of their position's merits, not on the basis of religious authority. That obligation does not change when they speak to public officials who happen to be Catholic.

8. The Future of Religion and Politics in America

As the *Mayflower* sailed toward the shores of the new land that would become America, it brought with it the two religious themes that would do battle throughout our history—religious idealism and religious intolerance. The Pilgrims fled from religious intolerance in England, but they also came to establish a new civil community "for the glory of God."

When the Founders gathered at the Constitutional Convention in Philadelphia, they could look back on a century-and-a-half of the battle between religious idealism and intolerance. On one side, they saw support for freedom, democracy, compassion, and a check on human frailty; on the other, they saw established religions and persecution for religious dissenters. They wanted to form a government which would curb religious intolerance without stifling religious idealism.

They drafted a constitution which provided a secular government for an essentially religious people. In the Constitution and the First Amendment, they took bold steps: they barred a religious test for federal office; they barred the establishment of a national religion and established the principle that government would not give any religion special treatment—either preference or persecution; they guaranteed the free exercise of religion.

The twin themes of religious idealism and intolerance continue to exist side by side today— with no sign that either will ever disappear. Religious idealism can be traced from the Great Awakening of the eighteenth century, which fostered values of democracy, to the efforts of religious leaders to reign in the nuclear arms race in the 1980s. Religious intolerance can be traced from the ban on public office for non-Protestants in many of the early colonies, to the Religious Right's effort to restrict public office to "Bible-believing, born-again" Christians.

One clear lesson of American history, which has been brought home with force in the past decade, is that it is simply a waste of time and energy to try to prevent "mixing religion and politics." They are inevitably mixed because both are part of the human condition. They are also mixed in an almost infinite variety of ways. Ronald Reagan and Walter Mondale hold diametrically opposed political views, but they are both motivated by a vision of the world shaped in part from their religious beliefs. Citizens become activists on both sides of issues from abortion to Zimbabwe because of values which stem from religious and moral values. Churches urge their members to become involved in the political process and urge public officials to take action. Members of various religious groups identify more strongly with one party than with the other, and candidates appeal to those groups as they would appeal to any other constituency. The way in which public officials handle the mixing of religion and politics itself becomes part of the record on which they are judged.

All of these themes are already at work as the process of selecting a new president in 1988 continues.

THE FUTURE OF THE RELIGIOUS RIGHT

One way to view the continued influence of religion on American politics is to consider a piece of conventional political wisdom: the belief that the Religious Right will not be a factor in the 1988 elections and beyond. There are three major reasons for this belief: 1) the Religious Right fared poorly in the 1986 elections, in which four of its major Senate supporters were turned out of office, eleven of twelve major candidates for House seats lost, and another House leader, Mark Siljander, was defeated in a primary; 2) Major Christian Right organizations, such as Christian Voice and the American Coalition for Traditional Values (ACTV) face financial difficulties; and 3) the public image of the televangelists was at a low point in 1987 in the wake of two major news stories: Oral Roberts's claim that God would take his life if he didn't raise the needed funds for his medical center, and the resignation of Jim and Tammy Bakker from the PTL ministry in the wake of scandal over Tammy's drug abuse and Jim's sexual encounter with a church secretary.

It would be foolish to argue that the Religious Right is not facing a difficult time. But the notion that the movement is moribund ignores some key facts.

First, despite all the bad publicity surrounding Roberts and the Bakkers, they were never visible political figures on the order of Jerry Falwell or Pat Robertson. Their problems do not automatically translate into problems for the more political televangelists. At the same time, while the fortunes of some televangelists have plummeted, the fortunes of others have soared; this group includes Jimmy Swaggart and D. James Kennedy, who have been politically active and are poised to take new leadership roles within the Religious Right.

A second factor is that, since 1985, the Religious Right has followed a grassroots strategy, targeting local school boards and party committees where they can have a disproportionate influence because of low visibility and voter turnout. This trend has developed independently of the fates of the leading Religious Right figures and shows every sign of continuing.

Third, this is not the first time that political pundits have written the movement's obituary. The Religious Right was dismissed as dead when it had no influence on the 1982 midterm elections, which were marked by Democratic victories in the wake of a recession. But it rebounded strongly in 1984. The movement is strongest when it is taken for granted and has the element of surprise on its side.

Finally, the Religious Right has become entrenched within the Republican Party and wields the same kind of influence like labor and feminists wield in the Democratic Party. Even if the public at large is turned off by the Religious Right in 1988, this doesn't mean that the Republican Party will be. Public opinion does not necessarily affect political structures and activities; the National Organization of Women was not at the heart of the public consensus in 1984, but it had a major influence on the Democratic Party that year. The same kind of dynamic is likely to be at work in the Republican Party in 1988. White Evangelicals are becoming the backbone of the Republican Party, and party leaders still try to reach this group by identifying with Religious Right leaders.

In fact, there are virtually no leading Republican candidates who have not tried to win the Religious Right's support. George Bush has sought and accepted Jerry Falwell's endorsement; he was disappointed when Jimmy Swaggart switches his support from Bush to Robertson; he has described his religious beliefs in a video to be viewed by Evangelical audiences.

Bush offered some timid criticisms of the Religious Right in a February 1987 speech to the National Religious Broadcasters. He told the Evangelicals, "Initially, you sought freedom. In the process, you gained power. And with power, a small minority now want control. There are those who would seek to impose their will and dictate their interpretations of morality on the rest of society." Bush singled out efforts to censor classroom reading of books like *Huckleberry Finn* and *The Diary of Anne Frank.*

But it was not "a small majority" of Religious Right leaders who were "trying to impose their interpretations of morality on the rest of society," it was the movement's top leadership—Pat Robertson, Tim and Beverly LaHaye, Jerry Falwell, Jimmy Swaggart, and Christian Voice.

And in supporting openness in education, Bush indulged in a bit of religious pandering that may have exceeded that of Ronald Reagan. "If you will permit me a very personal, unofficial observation," he said, "I'll tell you my basis for believing in this openness. I believe the pursuit of truth will always lead to Christ, who is the truth."

A rival of Bush's for the 1988 nomination is Representative Jack Kemp of New York. Kemp has criticized Robertson for making a partisan appeal to religion, but Kemp himself has strong Religious Right ties—he serves on the congressional advisory board of Christian Voice, and is the publisher of the *Biblical Scoreboard.* Christian Voice has been pushing Kemp hard within the Evangelical community. In early 1985, Kemp sought to beef up his credentials with the Religious Right by telling an ACTV conference that "God is the author of the US Constitution."

Senate Minority Leader Robert Dole and former Delaware governor Pierre DuPont reached out to Religious Right groups as their campaigns to win the Republican nomination for president began. But the major Religious Right figure within the Republican Party continues to be Pat Robertson himself. Through the first half of 1987, Robertson led all other candidates in money raised and number of volunteers. Bush conceded that Robertson had gathered more delegates in the complicated 1986 Michigan party caucuses, and Robertson forces came very close to taking over control of the Republican Party in South Carolina.

Robertson has never been in double figures among Republicans polled on their presidential preference, and a large majority of Republican Evangelicals oppose his candidacy. But money, organization, and zealous volunteers can have a great impact in political caucuses. Robertson showed in 1986 that his people could dominate Republican party conventions in Iowa, and that was obviously a dry run for 1988. It is entirely conceivable that a combination of low turnout, apathy toward politics in the wake of the Iran-Contra scandal, lack of enthusiasm for Bush and Dole, and a well-coordinated effort by Fundamentalist and Pentecostal churches could produce a strong finish or even a win for Robertson in key caucuses and primaries. Such a development would cause chaos within the party, and while Robertson could never win the nomination, he could play a significant role in determining who does. Republicans would face the same dilemma with Robertson that the Democrats faced with Jesse Jackson in 1984: trying to benefit from new voters he would bring into the party without threatening those already in. There's no reason to think they could do a better job than the Democrats did.

On the Democratic side, the 1988 crop of presidential candidates looks very much like the 1984 crop in one key respect—it, too, could pass as a church choir. Those joining Jesse Jackson and Gary Hart, who re-entered the race in December, 1987, in quest of the nomination include the son of Lutheran missionaries (Senator Paul Simon of Illinois); a graduate of Vanderbilt Divinity School (Senator Albert Gore, Jr., of Tennessee); and a host of other candidates comfortable with the rhetoric of values—former Arizona governor Bruce Babbitt, Governor Michael Dukakis of Massachusetts, and Representative Richard Gephardt of Missouri.

THE PARTIES AND RELIGION

One expression of the religious impulse in American politics is found in the major political parties themselves. There are two major strands of religious belief in America. One is Evangelical-Individualism, with a focus on individual freedom, personal piety, and sexual morality. This theme is found among the conservative religious activists, such as those described in the *Faith and Ferment* study of Minnesota Christians active in fighting abortion, pornography, gay rights, and so on. Those motivated by this theme have increasingly found themselves at home in the Republican Party. Conservative Evangelicals and mainstream Republicans share a common faith in the power of the individual and a conviction of the dangers of big government. But there is considerable tension between many conservative Evangelicals and mainstream Republicans who place a lower priority on the "social issues"; it may well be that the Reagan coalition was one that only Ronald Reagan could hold together.

The second major religious theme in America is Communal-Activism, represented by the activists in the *Faith and Ferment* study who were involved in the peace movements, civil rights, housing programs, and so on. This group has traditionally been at home in the Democratic Party.

Both themes are legitimate expressions of American religion, but feelings run strong between those in each camp. When Democrats are in power, conservative activists complain that they abandon "traditional values." When Republicans are in power, liberal activists complain that they have abandoned the values of fairness and compassion. Neither party's victory pushes values out of the public arena; they just give one set of values temporary priority over the other.

On a practical level, the political pendulum is swinging back toward the Communal-Activist values. There is growing concern about the spread of greed (Wall Street insider trading), violent racism (the death of a young black man in Howard Beach, New York), and government deception (the Iran-Contra scandal). During the Reagan era, the Republicans were able to link the rhetoric of values and piety. But events have decoupled the two; the Republicans find themselves left with the rhetoric of piety as the Democrats seek to claim a monopoly on the language of values with a call for public morality and a renewed commitment to the common good—at a time when the public mood is shifting from an individualistic to communitarian mode. (Gary Hart's initial decision to drop out of the 1988 race after revelations about his private meetings with a twenty-nine-year-old model and the decision of Senator Joseph Biden of Delaware to drop his presidential bid after revelations of his plagiarism magnified the emphasis on "character" and "values" in choosing a new president.)

There is another difference between the two parties in terms of religious rhetoric. The Republicans constantly speak of hope, pride, and growth. The Democrats, on the other hand, too often speak in the social gospel language of guilt and repentance. Whatever the merits of these latter characteristics in theology, they make bad politics: Americans like to be told that they can do good and can do better; but they don't like to be told that they've done wrong.

The two parties have one thing in common, however: both fail the American people by offering an inadequate philosophy of relating religion to politics. Two centuries after the ratification of the Constitution, Americans have a right to expect both major parties to understand the American tradition of mixing politics, but neither party meets that expectation.

The parties fail in very different ways. The Republicans rightly understand that religion is important to Americans, including in their political lives. But they have pandered to religion, debasing it in the process: Ronald Reagan's rhetoric consistently paid homage to one narrow vision of Christianity, leaving the implication that those outside that faith were less than Americans (Reagan declared May 7, 1987, a National Day of Prayer and appointed two Fundamentalists—Jerry Falwell and Bill Bright—as cochairman of the event); the 1984 Republican convention was dominated by partisan expressions of religion, Reagan's implication that those who disagreed with his policies were antireligion and claims to speak "as leaders under God's authority"; in 1986, Republican officials financed ads implying that the party supported a "personal relationship with Christ" and a letter attacking a Jewish congressman for raising money from Jews outside his district and then urged support for one candidate because her husband was Jewish and for another because his Jewish opponent's children were raised as Protestants. Republican leaders have made a mockery of the First Amendment and the ban on a religious test for office.

The Democrats have been eloquent in attacking the Republicans' partisan use of religion and warning of the dangers of identifying one party and one set of policies with the will of God. But, with rare exceptions, they have failed to offer a positive vision of the mixing of religion and politics; they have not talked about the appropriate ways in which religious individuals and institutions can be involved in political life. That failure would be bad enough if the Democrats were, in fact, a party of "secular humanists"—but they're not; most leading Democrats base their political platform on a religious vision. A Walter Mondale can say he went into politics because of his faith, without spelling out what that means. A Geraldine Ferraro can claim that Reagan is not a "good Christian" because of his budget cuts and then argue that religious beliefs are purely private—and not see the contradiction. A Paul Kirk can turn a legitimate political attack on Pat Robertson into a self-defeating and gratuitous attack upon millions of Evangelical Americans—many of whom are Democrats.

Americans deserve better than a choice between a party which panders to religion and a party which treats it like a taboo.

RELIGION AND CIVIL RELIGION

In many ways, the lengthy, complicated debate over mixing religion and politics boils down to a one question: Is religion good for American politics?

There are some simple—and wrong—answers to this question. For some people, religion is good for politics if it's on my side, and bad if it's on your side. Some people treat religion as a consistently benevolent force which deserves an honored place in political life; others treat it as a source of bigotry, hatred, and division.

Religion, of course, is both, and no theory about mixing religion and politics can succeed unless it recognizes that. We often hear today that those who do not subscribe to a particular set of sectarian beliefs have turned their backs on values. That is a lie.

The truth is that the vast majority of Americans subscribe to a set of shared values contained in the American civil religion. This civil religion does not have a detailed chatechism or canon law; instead, it embodies the ideals of freedom, democracy, justice, and equality which have shaped our nation's history—even when we have not lived up to them. It's easy to see the civil religion in practice: it was because of that civil religion that when Jerry Falwell called Bishop Desmond Tutu a phony, it was Falwell, not Tutu, who plummeted in public esteem; it was because of the civil religion that Americans watched their televisions and rooted for Corazon Aquino, not Ferdinand Marcos; it was because of that civil religion that Ronald Reagan suffered the largest one-month drop in popularity in the fifty-year history of the Gallup Poll after the revelation that his administration had sold arms to Iranian terrorists holding American hostages and sent some of the proceeds to the Nicaraguan Contras.

Religion is good for American politics when it supports the civil religion: when it speaks out with civility and respect; when it accepts the principles of tolerance and pluralism; when it appeals to a shared sense of morality and not to religious authority or doctrine; when it reminds us that we are a community, not a collection of isolated individuals; when it reminds us that we are our brothers' and sisters' keepers.

Religion is bad for American politics when it undermines the civil religion: when it speaks of political matters with the certitude of faith in a pluralistic society in which faith cannot be used as a political standard; when it treats opponents as agents of Satan; when it weakens a sense of national community; when it violates the precept of the Virginia Statute for Religious Freedom which formed the basis for the First Amendment—the precept that any American should no more be treated any differently than any other American on the basis of his or her opinions about religion than on the basis of his or her opinions on literature or geometry. That is only common sense.

Sources and Related Books, Articles, Speeches, and Documents

It would be impossible to list all of the sources used for this book. Most of the references are identified in the text. Much of the material concerning the 1984 and 1986 elections is based on primary source material—campaign documents, news clippings, and so forth, which are on file at People for the American Way (PFAW) in Washington, D.C. Quotes from Pat Robertson on the "700 Club" come from transcripts prepared by the PFAW staff. Some quotations transcribed from video recordings do not include all of the speaker's words, since spoken and written styles are often different. The following are sources of particular note:

Austin, Charles. "Role of Religion in American Political Life Can be Seen in Backgrounds of the Candidates." Religious News Service, February 8, 1984.

Bellah, Robert N., Richard Madsen, William M. Sullivan, Ann Swidler and Stephen M. Tipton. *Habits of the Heart: Individualism and Commitment in American Life.* Berkeley: University of California Press, 1985.

Bennett, William. Remarks to Knights of Columbus, August 17, 1985.

Benson, Peter, and Dorothy Williams. *Religion on Capitol Hill: Myths and Realities.* New York: Harper & Row, 1982.

Bernardin, Joseph. Remarks at Georgetown University, October 25, 1984.

Blumenthal, Sidney. "The Right's Quest for Law From a Mythical Past." *Washington Post,* November 3, 1985.

Bole, William. "Is the G.O.P. Becoming God's Own Party?" Religious News Service, as published in *Church and State,* January 1985.

Brennan, William. Remarks at Georgetown University, October 12, 1985.

Buie, Jim, and Al Menendez. "Here I Am, Send Me." *Church and State,* January 1984.

Bush, George. Remarks to National Religious Broadcasters, February 4, 1985.

Cannon, Lou. "The Lord Seems to Have Been Tapped as Reelection Chairman." *Washington Post,* February 13, 1984.

Chittister, Joan, and Martin Marty. *Faith and Ferment: An Interdisciplinary Study of Christian Beliefs and Practices.* Minneapolis: Augsburg Press and Liturgical Press, 1985.

Commager, Henry Steele. *Free Inquiry,* Vol. III, No. 3, Buffalo, NY

Committee for the Study of the American Electorate. "Non-Voter Study '84-'85." Washington, DC

Cox, Harvey. *Religion in the Secular City: Toward a Post-Modern Theology.* New York: Simon and Schuster, 1984.

Cuomo, Joe. "Ronald Reagan and the Prophecy of Armageddon." WBAI-FM, New York, NY, 1984.

Cuomo, Mario. Remarks at Cathedral of St. John the Divine, November 27, 1984.

———. Remarks at University of Notre Dame, September 13, 1987.

Dugger, Ronnie. "Does Reagan Expect a Nuclear Armageddon?" *Washington Post,* April 8, 1984.

Edsall, Thomas. "Onward, GOP Christians, Marching to '88." *Washington Post,* June 30, 1985.

Goldman, Ari L. "New York's Controversial Archbishop." *New York Times Magazine,* October 14, 1984.

Greider, William. "Attack of the Christian Soldiers." *Rolling Stone,* May 9, 1985.

Griffith, Emlynn. Remarks to National School Boards Association, January 22, 1987.

Hadden, Jeffrey, and Anson Shoupe, et al. "Why Jerry Falwell Killed the Moral Majority," in *The Godpumpers: Religion in the Electronic Age.* Bowling Green: University Popular Press, 1987.

Kennedy, Edward. Remarks at Liberty Baptist College, October 3, 1983.

Lang, Andrew. "President Reagan and Armageddon Ideology." Washington, DC: Christic Institute, 1984.

Lovin, Robin W., ed. *Religion and American Public Life.* Mahwah, NJ: Paulist Press, 1986.

Marty, Martin E. *Pilgrims in Their Own Land.* New York: Little, Brown, 1984.

McBrien, Richard P. *Caeser's Coin: Religion and Politics in America.* New York: Macmillan, 1987.

McPherson, Myra. "Gary Hart: Long Road From Kansas," *Washington Post,* March 20, 1984.

Meese, Edwin. Remarks to Federal Bar Association, September 13, 1985.

———. Remarks to Dickinson College, September 17, 1985.

———. Remarks to Knights of Columbus, August 7, 1985.

Menendez, Albert J. *Religion at the Polls.* Philadelphia: Westminster Press, 1977.

———. "Religion at the Polls 1986." *Church and State,* December 1986.

———. "No Religious Test: The Story of Our Constitution's Forgotten article." Silver Spring, MD: Americans United for Separation of Church and State, 1987.

Miller, William Lee. *The First Liberty: Religion and the American Republic.* New York: Alfred A. Knopf, 1985.

———. "The Seminarian Strain." *New Republic,* July 9, 1984.

Mondale, Walter. Remarks to B'nai B'rith International Convention, September 6, 1984.

Neuhaus, Richard John. *The Naked Public Square.* Grand Rapids, MI: Eerdmans, 1984.

New York Times. "Reagan's Religious 'We'." February 17, 1984.

Noll, Mark A., Nathan O. Hatch, and George M. Mardsen. *The Search for Christian America.* Westchester, IL: Crossway Books, 1983.

Reagan, Ronald. Remarks to National Prayer Breakfast, January 31, 1985.

———. Remarks to National Religious Broadcasters, January 30, 1984.

———. Remarks to National Religious Broadcasters, February 4, 1985.

———. Remarks to National Association of Evangelicals, March 6, 1984.

———. Remarks at Dallas Prayer Breakfast, August 23, 1984.

Reichley, A. James. *Religion in American Public Life.* Washington, DC: The Brookings Institution, 1985.

Robertson, Pat. Remarks at Yale University Law School, March 25, 1986.

Rothenberg, Stuart and Frank Newport. *The Evangelical Voter: Religion and Politics in America.* The Institute for Government and Politics, 1984.

Schmaltz, Jeffrey. "2,000 Catholics Lobby Leaders in Albany Visit." *New York Times,* March 10, 1987.

Schneider, William. "Half a Realignment." *New Republic,* December 3, 1984.

Schwartz, Herman. "The New Right's Court Packing Campaign." Washington, DC: People for the American Way, 1985.

Singer, David. "American Jews as Voters: The 1986 Elections." New York: American Jewish Committee.

Stevens, John Paul. Remarks to Federal Bar Association, October 23, 1985.

Index